BRITISH GOVERNMENT FINANCE

BRITISH GOVERNMENT FINANCE

BY

THE RT. HON. JOHN W. HILLS, M.P.
FORMERLY FINANCIAL SECRETARY
TO THE BRITISH TREASURY

AND

E. A. FELLOWES

THE SECOND EDITION
REVISED AND ENLARGED

NEW YORK M·CM·XXXII
COLUMBIA UNIVERSITY PRESS

LONDON: PHILIP ALLAN

Published in Great Britain by
Philip Allan under the title
"The Finance of Government"

First edition	*1925*
Second edition, revised and enlarged	*1932*

Printed in Great Britain

CONTENTS

PART I. REVENUE & ADMINISTRATION

PART II. CURRENCY

PART III. DEBT

PART I

REVENUE AND ADMINISTRATION

CHAPTER I

INTRODUCTION

THE ordinary man, whether he reads of mysterious proceedings such as the Appropriation Bill in Parliament, or whether he sees in *The Times* that borrowings on Ways and Means Advances amounted to so many millions, is inclined to think that our financial system is a fantastic jumble of absurdities. He may go further, and, frowning over his income tax return, may believe that those in authority are intentionally keeping it so, solemnly intoning an empty creed, designed to bemuse the vulgar, to keep them in ignorance of their rights, and thereby to extract an undue sum from their pockets. He is mistaken. Though some of our procedure is antiquated and has ceased to have meaning, and some more, once of essential utility, is being clumsily adapted to purposes for which it is ill suited, it is neither absurd nor misleading. Intricate our system is, and must be, as are all attempts to apply broad general principles to the infinite complexities of life and of affairs ; but illogical it is not. It is capable of improvement, like other human institutions : but the main outline of its structure will probably remain unchanged.

To make clear the intricacies of this system, and to explain its machinery, is the business of this book. It is designed to show the system in working, and incidentally it is hoped to prove that much which looks irrational, or designed to puzzle or to deceive, is nothing but the working out of accepted principles.

The difficulties, however, which beset the ordinary man in his attempt to understand the business of public finance are not due solely to the complexity of the machinery ; they arise also from a misconception of its nature. This misconception has been fostered by the use of false analogies, that most dangerous method of reasoning. Volumes could be written on the errors into which the human mind has fallen through explaining the state by analogy either with a machine or with a man or with an organism. It is none of them : it is not a mechanism, nor is it man writ large : and in the same way its finance is not comparable with that of a well-managed business or with that of a prudent father of a family, with both of which it is so often compared, with tiresome iteration.

A business tries to make profits. The state makes no profits. A business keeps down expenses in order to increase its income : the state keeps down expenses in order to diminish its income. There is not analogy here, but contradiction, and the same is the case if you take the symbolism of the prudent citizen. He earns an income, keeps out of debt, makes wise investments, and spends the balance. The state does the reverse. It earns little, is never out of debt, and makes practically no investments. The individual spends what he gets. The state gets what it spends. He is conditioned by his income, the state by its expenditure.

These are no verbal dialectics, but the statement of a truth so obvious as to be a commonplace. And yet false analogies lead one to overlook it.

They lead their followers into strange places; to the idea that the state's income is like that of a business, or that it can congratulate itself if it obtains a high yield from the beer duty, just as an individual can congratulate himself on developing a property. It is looked upon as an increase of wealth. It is forgotten that more money received by the state means so much less money in the pockets of the people. The state does not earn money, but takes it. It should not take more than it needs, for its income is a burden upon its subjects. The justification and the measure of this burden must be the value of the services provided. A state is not prosperous when its income is great, but when its expenditure is wise and efficient, and when the benefits from that expenditure outweigh the load imposed by its income. Taxable capacity must only come in to fix the outside limit. If we proceed otherwise, we approach national finance from the wrong end. Incidentally we run the danger of thinking that the more the state can raise the more prosperous it is. And when we have reached that point, we are putting out upon a sea to which there is no shore.

This misconception of the relative positions of state income and expenditure is not confined to the man in the street. We find it in parliamentary procedure. Too little attention is paid to expenditure. Estimates, if discussed at all, are debated in a House which is empty and languid. On the other hand, taxation, the raising of the money, excites keen interest and controversy. And no doubt it is right that it should. But it is forgotten that the amount of taxation is fixed by expenditure. And about half of this expenditure is never even discussed in the House of Commons, but is fixed by the government without criticism.

And now for an account, and it will be short, of what our national expenditure and income consist of. We are not concerned with the amount of expenditure, only with the manner in which it is authorised and paid ; nor with the system under which the country is taxed, only with the method by which taxes are collected. Free trade or protection, capital levy or a tax on land values, reach our ears only as confused murmurs from distant battlefields. All that need be said is that a state spends money on the army, navy, and air force, on interest on, and redemption of, debt, on education, on health, on housing, on the hundred and one activities of a government.

The money to meet this expenditure is found in four ways : either from the yield of certain assets, or from fees for services, or out of taxes, or by borrowing. The first two are its only true revenue. They come from many sources. The state receives dividends on investments, such as shares in the Suez Canal and Anglo-Persian Oil Company. The Commissioners of Woods, Forests and Land Revenues collect the rents of its mines, its farms and its houses. The Post Office carries our letters, and its net income is revenue of the state. We receive payments from foreign nations, such as the Boxer indemnity from China, or the Reparations which Germany pays. The Disposals Board sells surplus stores ; and there are many more receipts, either for goods or services, permanent or temporary. These together constitute the state's revenue, and its only revenue. But they pay only a fraction of our expenditure. Most of it is met out of taxes, and they, both from their amount, and from social, political and psychological reasons too obvious to need statement, engage most of our activities and controversies. All imposts in every state, whether free trade or protectionist, communist or individualist, fall into two broad classes. They are either direct or indirect. Our business is collection and payment only, and we shall see that a different method is adopted in each case.

After this glance at the nature of the national expenditure and income, the next questions to be considered are who, in fact, decides what shall be spent each year, and how the necessary money is raised. In constitutional countries, finance is the affair partly of the legislature, partly of the executive. The legislature authorises expenditure and imposes taxes ; the executive collects the money and pays the bill. That is the theory, but the practice in the United Kingdom is rather different. First of all, in financial questions, the legislature, in fact, has ceased to be the Crown, Lords and Commons, and become the House of Commons and that House alone. In the past taxation was the prerogative of kings, but after a long series of struggles, beginning with Magna Charta and ending with the passage of the Bill of Rights, Lords and Commons received the right of granting or refusing taxation. Another struggle for financial domination, which had, in fact, been in progress for some hundreds of years, then came more prominently into view – a struggle between the two Houses which has only been ended in modern times. As far back as the reign of Henry IV the Commons claimed the sole right to grant taxation. By the famous resolution of 1678 they further claimed that the Lords had no right to alter bills for aids and supplies, a claim which the Lords denied in theory but admitted in practice. Such was the position during the eighteenth century, and meanwhile, after 1688, the Commons had finally secured the right of deciding for what purposes the money granted should be spent. After the rejection of the paper duties by the Lords in 1860, the Commons made a practice of consolidating all the taxes for the year into one bill, the Finance Bill, and the Lords never dared to upset the whole financial scheme of the year until in 1909 the Finance Bill was rejected on second reading. The Parliament Act of 1911 followed, and the right of the Lords to reject a Finance Bill has to all intents and purposes disappeared.

It is therefore an anachronism to talk of the control of Parliament over finance : the control is that of the House of Commons alone. But to talk of the power of the House of Commons is almost as misleading, for it has little power against the government. Its power over it, in theory absolute, is slight in practice. A private member of the House can criticise expenditure, or move to reduce it, he cannot move to increase it or to authorise a new commitment. He can criticise a tax or move to lower it, or in certain conditions move to substitute one tax for another ; he cannot move to increase it or to levy a new one. This is the prerogative of the government alone. This rule is founded on sound financial sense, as will be shown later : what must be noted at the moment is the immense power it gives governments over the House of Commons. This power is further enhanced by the convention whereby governments treat all questions of expenditure as matters of confidence, and if they are beaten on such a question they resign. This, though it looks like accepting the decision of the House, in reality overrides it : for supporters of a government, who know that if they defeat it they will turn it out, are reluctant to do so. In practice, therefore, the House accepts the financial proposals of the government. Thus, though it is theoretically permissible to point to the divided function of legislature and executive, the first allowing the expenditure and levying the impost, the second gathering the cash and paying it out, you have not told the whole truth, unless at the same time the meaning of the term legislature is explained and the power of governments shown. The government is the executive : they dominate the legislature ; and the long battle, which began by refusing to one executive – the Crown – all financial powers, has ended by surrendering these powers to another executive, the Cabinet. A different executive, truly : a body elected by a suffrage nearly universal. But still, an executive and a powerful one, more powerful than any Plantagenet or Tudor sovereign. Over expenditure the executive is supreme. Its powers over taxation are less absolute, as we shall see.

It is perhaps as well at this point to state exactly the powers, such as they are, of the Crown and House of Lords over finance, in order not to have to mention the matter again. No expenditure or tax can be initiated except by the Crown, which of course acts through its ministers, nor is that expenditure or tax finally valid until enshrined in an Act of Parliament, and an act has to pass the Upper as well as the Lower House and to receive the royal assent. Such royal assent, however, is never in practice withheld, and in our constitutional monarchy and under our wise sovereigns it is inconceivable that it ever should be withheld. The powers of the House of Lords, again, are strictly limited by the Parliament Act, 1911. Under that act, all money bills which reach the House of Lords one month at least before the end of the session, and are not passed by it within one month of receipt, can receive the royal assent and become acts over the heads of the House of Lords. The term money bill includes all measures dealing only with finance, or kindred or subordinate subjects, and the question whether any particular measure comes within this definition is decided by the Speaker, after consultation with two of the senior members of the House of Commons. It will be noticed that, in order to fall within the Parliament Act and to become law against the will of the House of Lords, a bill must be entirely financial. Hence two interesting consequences. On the one hand, some Finance Bills which included certain non-financial provisions have not been certified as ' money bills ' under the Parliament Act by the Speaker, while many other bills have come within this definition.[1] The Parliament Act makes, as it was intended to make, the House of Lords powerless in finance. At the most it can hold up a ' money bill ' for a month. At the end of that time the bill is presented for royal assent and becomes law over the heads of a recalcitrant House of Lords, although in fact this power has never had to be used.

There are certain other pieces of financial procedure in which the Crown still has to play a part.

[1] Appendix I. gives a list of the Finance Bills, both certified and uncertified, and also a list of the titles of bills other than Finance Bills which have been certified as money bills.

The sovereign, in theory, still has the sole right of initiating expenditure, and no proposition involving a charge on the revenue can be brought before the House of Commons unless a Privy Councillor, acting for the sovereign, signifies the royal consent to the proposition in question. Moreover, as that part of the yearly expenditure technically known as Supply is granted to the Crown, a royal order is necessary before any moneys can be issued from the Exchequer. The last process is, however, now purely formal.

All expenditure made by the state is authorised by Parliament at some time or another. Some expenditure is authorised every year. This is the current expenditure of the departments, expenditure on what are called Supply Services. Other expenditure of a more permanent character, upon what are called Consolidated Fund Services, is paid out of the Consolidated Fund year by year, but is imposed by an Act of Parliament which authorises the payment until the act lapses or is repealed. After expenditure has been authorised, and taxes imposed, by legislation, finance passes out of the hands of the House of Commons into those of the executive. The various spending departments carry out the work for which Parliament has granted them money. The Admiralty builds ships ; and the Home Office inspects factories ; the Ministry of Health subsidises house-building. On the other side of the account, the great revenue offices, the Board of Inland Revenue and the Board of Customs and Excise, collect taxes and pay them into the Consolidated Fund at the Bank of England. This fund represents the income of the state, and in theory all receipts go into it and all payments are made out of it. In practice there are exceptions, as we shall see. The Comptroller and Auditor-General, who is a high official, responsible directly to the House of Commons, sees that not a shilling is issued from the fund beyond the amount that has been authorised by Parliament. No payments are made directly out of the Consolidated Fund, but the Comptroller and Auditor-General, at the instance of the Treasury, authorises the issue of the money required to the Paymaster-General. This official sees that the spending departments of state receive the stream of cash and credit necessary to carry on the country's business. Of great importance in this scheme of administration is the part played by the Treasury which fills the rôle of financial expert. All through the year it supervises the expenditure of the departments. Working in close touch with them, it discusses their programmes, criticises their costs and lays down rules for financial administration. Finally, at the end of the year – and our financial years end awkwardly enough on 31st March – the spending departments close their accounts. Expenditure and receipts are brought together, and there is a final balance and audit. If departments have outrun the constable, they must come humbly to Parliament and endeavour to get their excesses legalised. If, on the other hand, they have underspent, they surrender their balances, with some exceptions, into the Consolidated Fund. On 31st March at four o'clock[1] in the afternoon the guillotine falls. Immediately the next year starts, each year being a separate, self-contained, watertight unit, and the ordered processes of our finance begin all over again.

[1] The exact hour of closing the national accounts on 31st March depends on the closing time of the Bank.

All expenditure and income are settled in advance for the coming year. The state has no capital account in the sense that a large business has one, though capital and income are separated for certain purposes. It may build a railway in Nyasaland out of income, it may sell war stores bought out of borrowed money and treat the proceeds as revenue. It has a national debt, and a big one, but this is not charged against its assets, which would not cover a fraction, but on taxes, actual or potential. And it has only one yearly balance sheet, for it does not follow the evil practice of some countries and separate its extraordinary or so-called non-recurrent expenditure from the ordinary; and at normal times it balances its budget without borrowing.

From the procedure, thus roughly outlined, certain broad principles emerge, some of them of wide social and political import, others matters only of good accountancy. To sum up:

First. The financial unit is the year commencing 1st April, ending 31st March, and all expenditure and income is estimated in advance.

Second. No expenditure can be authorised or tax levied except on the motion of the government (acting for the Crown) and with the assent of the House of Commons.

Third. Money can only be spent on the object for which it has been voted.

Fourth. All receipts must be paid into, and all payments made out of, a single fund, the Consolidated Fund or the Exchequer Account. This rule has many exceptions.

Fifth. In normal times the yearly accounts

should balance, and recourse to borrowing to effect this balance should be avoided.

Sixth. Money unspent at the end of the year must be surrendered. There are exceptions to this.

These are the principles on which the financial system of Great Britain is based. They are sound, in that misapplication of money is nearly impossible, that financial stability is assured, and that the exact position at any given moment can be easily ascertained, since there are no concealed assets or liabilities.[1] Its weaknesses will be dealt with after the system has been reviewed in detail. With this brief and general introduction it is now possible to proceed to a closer examination of the financial machine, and of the men by whom that machine is worked.

[1] It is worthy of note that a departure from these rules by which in particular the Unemployment Insurance Fund became in fact a concealed liability led to an unbalanced budget which in turn was the cause of the financial crisis of 1931.

CHAPTER II

THE EXECUTIVE

THE government, as has been shown, controls Parliament, or it ceases to be the government. It is also the head of our great civil service, which acts under the direction of its parliamentary chiefs. Both the rules which govern our civil service, and the character of the men who run it, must be carefully understood if we are properly to appreciate the system in working. Good rules are necessary, but so are good men ; each react on the other, and, before explaining the organisation, a word must be said of those who operate it. The civil service works behind closed doors. It indulges neither in propaganda nor in defence. Its merits are often claimed by politicians and its mistakes often visited on its own head. The integrity of the civil service and its sense of duty are too well known to need emphasis. But what is not always recognised is its business capacity and common sense. Indeed, it is often accused of the opposite defects of being apt to be bound by rule, and of regarding the form as more important than the substance. This is untrue, as all who know the service must recognise ; and much of such criticism is due to ignorance of the nature of government, and of the qualities it requires in its servants. Throughout the whole civil service runs a spirit, difficult to put into words, but unmistakable to everyone who has met it, of sanity and of balance, whilst those at the head of it are men of quite exceptional ability.

The work to be done by the state is carried out by the various departments, War Office, Board of Education, Home Office and so on. Most of these have a direct parliamentary chief, and in the case of all the great spending departments, such as army, navy, Ministry of Health and others, he is a member of the Cabinet.[1] Under him, the office is staffed by civil servants who do not change with governments. This dual constitution, a civil service permanent and technical, under a politician who is transitory and usually an amateur, must always be remembered.

But each department is not a watertight unit: it forms part of a larger whole. The expenditure of each is conditioned by the general scheme of expenditure put forward by the executive and authorised by the House of Commons. The Cabinet is at the head of the executive, and the Prime Minister sitting in Downing Street has to reconcile the views of his colleagues, who want to spend, with those of the Chancellor of the Exchequer, who wants to save. The Chancellor of the Exchequer corresponds to the continental Minister of Finance, although, with that fondness for preserving the pomp and circumstance of the past so characteristic of the British people, the Treasury is still nominally ruled by My Lords of the Treasury, and its letters still express the opinions of Their Lordships. But this is no more than a picturesque survival, though it is important

[1] The Minister of Health was the only representative of the big spending departments in the Cabinet of the first National Government, which was, however, reduced to half the size of a normal Cabinet, and which was comparable to the war Cabinets rather than to that of an ordinary government. On the reconstruction of the government after the general election of 1931, the Cabinet reverted to its normal size and constitution.

that the Prime Minister, in his capacity of First Lord, is closely connected with the Treasury which is the most important of the departments of state.

It is the Treasury's business generally to supervise the finance of the country. It watches and co-ordinates the expenditure of the various departments; it considers taxation and prepares the budget, and it is responsible for the terms for raising and repayment of all loans. Grouped round the Treasury, and assisting it in these various tasks, are many important offices. There is the Board of Inland Revenue, under a chairman who rules over Somerset House and collects all direct taxes, and the Board of Customs and Excise, housed in Lower Thames Street, also under its chairman. Then there is the Mint, under a Deputy Master (the Chancellor of the Exchequer is titular master); the Public Trustee; the Public Works Loan Board; the National Savings Committee; and, strangely enough in such lofty company, the Stationery Office. Of more importance is the National Debt Office, in Old Jewry. It is under a Comptroller, a civil servant. The National Debt Office does not manage the national debt: that is done by the Bank of England; it buys and sells government stocks, and invests money for such government departments as possess it. Of all these offices the Chancellor of the Exchequer is political chief, and either he, or more usually the Financial Secretary to the Treasury, answers all questions concerning them in the House of Commons. The Commissioners of Woods and Forests are also responsible to the Treasury, and the Pay Office is another department under Treasury control. The titular head of the department is the Paymaster-General, who is a minor minister; but he is unpaid, and has no connection with the work of the office. The Assistant Paymaster-General, a civil servant, is the real head of the department, and he is under the direct supervision of the Treasury.

Turning to the internal organisation of the Treasury itself, the formal nature of the departmental work of the majority of the Lords of the Treasury has already been commented on. Indeed, the Junior Lords, together with the Parliamentary Secretary to the Treasury, are in fact the government whips in the House of Commons. The real head of the Treasury is the Chancellor of the Exchequer, and his political assistant is the Financial Secretary to the Treasury. It may easily be imagined that the Chancellor is, next to the Prime Minister, the most important member of the Cabinet, a position perhaps symbolised by his residence at No. 11 Downing Street.[1] The office of Financial Secretary is also much sought after. The post is usually given to a youngish man marked out for promotion to Cabinet rank in the near future, and no better test of ability could be desired. The Financial Secretary has wide original powers, all financial business traversing his room and much of it being settled there without further question. In the House of Commons much of the routine work falls to his lot, and he can do much to relieve the burden that of necessity falls on his chief during the passage of the budget. Though not in the Cabinet, his office is recognised as next in importance to those held by members of that august assembly.

Under the Chancellor and the Financial Secretary

[1] At the moment (1932) the Lord President of the Council occupies No. 11 Downing Street, but this is exceptional.

the chief of the Treasury is the Permanent Secretary to the Treasury, a civil servant and the head of the whole civil service. He is chief-of-staff to the Chancellor. Under him the Treasury is organised into two departments, Finance and Supply Services and Establishments, each under a Controller. The Establishments Department deals, as its name implies, with personnel, not of the Treasury alone, but of the whole civil service. The Controller of this department must give his consent before any department can increase its staff even by one writing assistant, and all rates of salary are considered by him.

The Controller of Finance and Supply Services, with two deputies to assist him, deals with all questions concerned with the budget and all matters coming under the heading of finance, while he also deals with all departmental estimates. This means that the Finance Department on the one hand supervises the national debt, the raising and repayment of loans, banking and currency problems and financial relations with Dominions and foreign countries, while on the other hand it also examines all the proposed national expenditure before submitting it to the House of Commons. It is a rule which should be invariable, but which some governments break, that no new scheme involving expenditure should be brought before the Cabinet until it has been discussed with the Chancellor of the Exchequer, and he has had time to examine it with the Permanent Secretary to the Treasury and the Controller of Finance and Supply Services. It may be feared that this gives the Treasury too much power, in that they will look at all schemes from the budgetary standpoint only, and disregard other issues. But this is not so. The thread of finance runs through all questions, but none are purely financial. This is well recognised, and Treasury criticism is on the broadest lines. Of course, it is only the major issues which go before the Cabinet, but all proposals involving any increase of expenditure, however small, must be submitted by the department concerned to the Treasury, where its merits are weighed and its cost considered. The process goes on throughout the year, the departments applying, the Controller judging and criticising, and it is only when Treasury sanction has been obtained that the proposals can be embodied in the estimates and laid before the House of Commons. Everyone who has had to do with a spending department knows how real and powerful is the control exercised by the Treasury. For the most part departments are content to abide by the Controller's decision, for his powers are large, and his influence, and that of his chief, the Permanent Secretary, wider still, so that appeals to the Chancellor are confined to the larger issues on which the Cabinet itself may have to pronounce the final decision.

Under each Controller is a large and highly skilled staff, for the Treasury obtains the pick of candidates for the civil service, and its organisation is exceedingly efficient. And remember, too, the position of the Financial Secretary to the Treasury, the Chancellor's deputy. It is in consultation with him, and subject to his approval, that the Controllers carry on their continuous and laborious work.

But although the Treasury keeps such a close watch over the departments, sees that public money is not misapplied, and lays down the broad principles of economy, it cannot be certain that from day to day the money is being spent in the most efficient manner. The Treasury can save the pounds, but to save the pence it must rely upon the departments themselves.

For the actual day-to-day spending of the money is in their hands, and it is their duty to lay it out in such a way as to provide most adequately the service for which it was granted by Parliament. It will be remembered that the parliamentary chief of an office brings, or ought to bring, to his work the invaluable qualities of common sense and the power of deciding between conflicting experts. That is one of the most admirable features of our political life, and few want to change it. But it has this corresponding disadvantage – that the politician usually starts with no technical knowledge of his departmental work and often with no business experience of running an office. He cannot, therefore, be relied upon to see that the money granted to his department is spent without waste. Under him is a Permanent Secretary, a civil servant who is his expert adviser, his chief-of-staff, and the head and ruler of the office, and it is on him that the real responsibility for efficient expenditure lies. As a rule[1] he is the Accounting Officer, and as such responsible to Parliament for the financial administration of the grant for the service of any department, for the proper conduct of its financial

[1] In 1932, the heads of all the principal departments were also the Accounting Officers, with the following exceptions : Post Office, where the Accountant-General is still the Accounting Officer, while in the Home Office and the Ministry of Health the Deputy Permanent Secretary is the Accounting Officer. In the Foreign Office there is a Finance Officer, while in the House of Commons the Clerk of the Fees is also Accounting Officer, and the Controller of Finance and Supply Services acts in that capacity for departments attached to the Treasury.

business, and for its efficient and economical financial administration. He is appointed by the Prime Minister after consultation with the Permanent Secretary to the Treasury and the political chief of the office concerned. The Accounting Officer signs the Appropriation Accounts, which are presented to the House of Commons after the end of the year, and thereby makes himself responsible for their correctness. Further, he is answerable for balances in the custody of the department, though, for the most part, these balances are not held by him, but are in the hands of sub-accountants. He must therefore see that adequate regulations are enforced to ensure their proper management, and must check the accounts and cash balances of the sub-accountants. All officers executing business of account and book-keeping, and all persons in charge of balances held by the department, are under his direct control and supervision. He cannot delegate his responsibility to them. He must himself allow all payments made by the department. Before making or allowing any payment, he must assure himself of the correctness and propriety of the transaction. As he cannot go into the details of every payment made, he is considered free of responsibility if he acts on certified statements made by the officers in charge of the detailed duties of account. He must, however, use his common sense and administrative experience in considering these statements, and in cases of serious doubt or difficulty he may consult the Treasury.

If the Accounting Officer is not the permanent head of the department he is not an independent critic. He is subordinate to the permanent head of his department, and may be directed by him to make a payment which he considers to be wrong. In such cases the Accounting Officer must send a written objection to his superior, giving reasons for his disagreement with the payment. If the order is then repeated in writing, he must obey it, but is freed from responsibility, which then rests with his superior.

There has been an increasing tendency recently to regard the Accounting Officer as closely concerned with questions of economy and not restricted to questions of regularity. This means that he criticises expenditure not only from the point of view of its technical correctness, but from that of financial policy.

It was with this end in view that in 1920 the Treasury decided to appoint, wherever possible, the permanent head of the department as Accounting Officer, as no one would be in a better position to secure economy and efficiency in expenditure. His power to criticise the merits, as distinct from the regularity of payments, is of great importance. He works in close touch with the Treasury, and they regard him as a valuable instrument for securing uniformity and economy. It is through the Accounting Officer also that the House of Commons is able to exercise control over the departments, for he has to appear before the Public Accounts Committee, and, as will be seen when the activities of that body are discussed, he may have to defend the action of his department before them. Their criticism, coupled with his personal responsibility, is a powerful check on the expenditure of departments.

In all the big departments the Accounting Officer has under him a Director of Establishments, who is an expert on all matters connected with the staff and their salaries, and an Accountant-General, who is an expert on finance, each of these officers having under them an expert staff.

The duties of the Accounting Officer have been described at what may appear to be undue length. The reason is that the importance of his office is hardly known, and that his responsibilities and power to effect economies are growing, and will grow further.

But it must not be forgotten that the executive must obtain the sanction of the legislature before money can either be collected or spent. The whole income of the state (with a very few exceptions) goes into the Consolidated Fund, and a government can only draw on that fund with the consent of the House and for the purposes which the House has decreed. The whole of the year's finance, however, is not voted afresh every year. The bulk of the expenditure is so voted on what are called estimates, prepared by the different spending departments. This annual expenditure is for services called Supply Services, and the business of getting it through Parliament is called Supply. It includes the cost of army, navy, air force and civil service. The expenditure which is authorised by permanent acts which do not need renewing, or by acts operating for stated periods, is for services called Consolidated Fund Services. They include interest on the national debt, the king's civil list, and salaries of judges. It is chiefly non-controversial, while, on the contrary, much controversy centres round Supply Services and the estimates on which they are based. Revenue also is partly yearly, partly permanent, but in proportions opposite to those of expenditure, for it is mainly permanent. Some comes in of itself, as do dividends on the Suez Canal and Anglo-Persian oil shares. But infinitely more comes from taxes, and about 60 per cent. even of tax revenue is permanent, resting on statutes which are not re-enacted yearly, the income tax and sur-tax being the only two important annual taxes now left.[1]

The financial year begins on 1st April, but preparations for that year have started many months in advance. All through the preceding summer there will have been those informal conversations between the spending departments and the Treasury as to their financial needs in the coming year, which precede the formulation of its probable requirements by each department, for no charge may be inserted in the estimates unless due authority has already been obtained. Much ground has therefore been cleared before the first formal step is taken, the issue by the Treasury of the Estimates Circular on 1st October. This calls for the forwarding of all estimates to the Treasury on or before a fixed date, usually 1st December, and directs attention to the necessity for economy. On their arrival at the Treasury the estimates are examined, and, if need be, amended, though the process of amendment may entail a further period of bargaining. This is particularly likely to occur in the case of estimates for the three fighting services. The navy, the army and the air force in the first instance submit only a total figure to the Treasury (civil departments submit their estimates in detail from the first), and allocate that figure between the votes as they please,

[1] Prior to 1929, when the tea duty was repealed, one direct and one indirect tax were voted annually. No indirect tax is now so voted.

so that in the main the detailed estimates do not come to the notice of the Treasury until the final draft is submitted for their approval. A serious dispute between the Treasury and one of these departments is likely to involve great issues of policy and large sums of money, and usually entails the intervention of the Cabinet, whereas, should big new expenditure be incurred on the civil services, as it has recently been incurred for derating, it does not make its first appearance in an estimate, but in a bill, and it is on the bill that the question of policy arises. Finally, when the estimates have been agreed, printed, signed by that member of the government who will present them to the House of Commons, they are presented, and circulated to members soon after the House meets early in the following year. The army, navy and air estimates are signed and presented by the Board of Admiralty, the Army Council, and the Air Council respectively, but all estimates for the civil services are signed and presented by the Financial Secretary to the Treasury.

Estimates are grouped under four heads, army, navy, air force, civil service and revenue departments. They are divided into items called votes, each comprising a particular service, e.g. police, or a group of services administered by a single department, e.g. colonial services. The unit of the vote runs throughout financial procedure. Each vote can be discussed separately, it is passed separately by the House of Commons, separately paid, and separately audited. Money cannot be transferred from one vote to another, except in the case of a vote for a fighting service, where such transfers are allowed, subject to Treasury sanction. These transfers are formally approved by the House of Commons after the close of the year.

Each vote is divided into three parts, of which the first specifies the service or purpose for which the estimate is presented, and the total amount of money required for that service. Part II divides that total into sub-heads, showing the amount of money estimated to be spent on, or received under, each sub-head. Part III is a detailed explanation of the expenditure or receipts making up the sub-heads of Part II. Part I is vitally important, for it alone is included in the Appropriation Act of the year, whereby Parliament authorises the payment of a specific sum for a specific purpose. Part II, which, together with Part I, will be reproduced in the Appropriation Account, shows the heads under which the Treasury requires the total sum mentioned in Part I to be accounted for. Savings on one sub-head may be set off against excesses on another, provided that Treasury sanction is obtained and that the total sum mentioned in Part I is not exceeded. Part III is for information only, and appears only in the estimate.

Part II of an estimate is drawn up in one column of contents and four of figures, the latter giving the sums required for the year, those for the previous year,[1] and the increases or the decreases ; the sums are then added up, and the result, whether more or less than the previous year, is shown in figures. Any chance revenue which may have fallen to the department, called an appropriation in aid, and shown in a separate sub-head, is deducted, and the net amount, corresponding, of course, to that shown

[1] That is, the original estimates for the previous year, not including supplementary estimates, unless, which is not normally the case, the latter have been sanctioned at the time these estimates are presented.

in Part I, is the sum demanded. Then there follow various explanations and amplifications. An actual estimate for the current year is here reproduced.

British Museum

I. ESTIMATE of the Amount required in the Year ending 31 March, 1932, to pay the Salaries and other Expenses of the British Museum, including a Grant in Aid (26 Geo. 2, c. 22; 41 & 42 Vict. c. 55; 57 & 58 Vict. c. 34; 2 Edw. 7, c. 12; 20 & 21 Geo. 5, c. 46; &c.).

One Hundred and Eighty-one Thousand Four Hundred and Seventy-one Pounds.

II. Sub-heads under which this Vote will be accounted for by the Trustees of the British Museum.

	1931.	1930.	Increase	Decrease
	£	£	£	£
A.—Salaries, Wages, and Allowances ..	134,582	141,333	—	6,751
B.—Police Pensioners and Police	6,725	6,715	10	—
C.—Purchases and Acquisitions (Grant in Aid)*	30,000	32,500	—	2,500
D.—Mounting, Preparing, &c.	1,705	1,705	—	—
E.—Printing, Photography, &c.	21,176	13,840	7,336	—
F.—Fire-Extinguishing Apparatus	250	250	—	—
G.—Furniture and Fittings	6,000	6,000	—	—
H.—Incidental Expenses	6,170	6,185	—	15
I.—Telephones	569	565	4	—
J.—Annuity in Respect of Loan for Purchase of Land (57 & 58 Vict. c. 34)	7,733	7,733	—	—
Gross Total .. .. .. £	214,910	216,826	7,350	9,266
Deduct:				
K.—Appropriations in Aid	33,439	20,292	—	13,147
Net Total .. .. £	181,471	196,534†	7,350	22,413
		Net Decrease ..	£15,063	

	£
† Total Original Net Estimate, 1930, British Museum	297,263
Add—Transfer from Class VI., 15	1,420
	298,683
Deduct—Transfer to Class IV., 3	102,149
	£196,534

* Expenditure out of this grant in aid will be accounted for in detail to the Comptroller and Auditor-General. Any balance of the sum issued which may remain unexpended at 31 March 1932 will not be liable to surrender to the Exchequer.

	1931.	1930.
The total expenditure in connection with this service is estimated as follows :	£	£
Gross Estimate above	214,910	216,826
Estimated amount (net) included in other Estimates in connection with this service :—		
Exchequer and Audit Department, Class I., 9	200	315
Buildings, furniture, fuel and light, &c., Class VII., 1 ..	105,060	100,395
" " " " Class VII., 7 ..	11,590	11,130
Rates, Class VII., 13	7,850	13,000
Stationery and Printing, Class VII., 14 :—		
Publications, Parliamentary and non-Parliamentary ..	100	50
Printing, paper, &c.	22,500	20,700
Office supplies	400	250
Superannuation, &c., Class VIII., 4	21,000	31,516
Post Office, Revenue Departments, No. 3	429	632
TOTAL EXPENDITURE .. .. .. £	384,039	394,814
The receipts in connection with this service are estimated as follows :—		
Appropriations in aid above .. .. £	33,439	20,292

III. DETAILS of the foregoing

A.—SALARIES, WAGES, AND ALLOWANCES : (*a*)

Numbers. 1930.	Numbers. 1931.	1. ADMINISTRATIVE, TECHNICAL, AND CLERICAL.		1931. £	1930. £
1	1	Director and Principal Librarian	(1,500*l*.)	1,640	1,686
9	9	Keepers of Departments	(1,000*l*.)	10,381	10,845
1	1	Secretary	(850*l*.–50*l*.–1,000*l*.)	1,153	1,205
9	9	Deputy Keepers of Departments ..	(900*l*)	9,666	9,973
1	1	Accountant	(500*l*.–20*l*.–600*l*.)	674	887
1	1	Assistant Secretary ..	(500*l*.–20*l*.–600*l*.)	724	743
53	55	Assistant Keepers, First Class (37) Assistant Keepers, Second Class (18)	(475*l*.–25*l*.–800*l*.) (250*l*.–20*l*.–290*l*.–25*l*.–440*l*.)	34,056	33,922
1	1	Staff Officer	(400*l*.–15*l*.–500*l*.)	528	672
12	12	Clerks, Higher Grade ..	(300*l*.–15*l*.–400*l*.)	5,742	6,114
1	1	Examiner of Binding ..	(250*l*.–15*l*.–350*l*.)	439	454
1	1	Hall Superintendent ..	(170*l*.–5*l*.–210*l*.)	244	259
1	1	Hall Clerk	(100*l*.–5*l*.–140*l*.)	224	246
—	—	Night Patrol, 15*s*. a week, to Hall Clerk or other official performing the duty (part of the year) ..		20	20

Here follow 5 more pages of the detailed expenditure but the contents of Part III are sufficiently exemplified by the extract here given.

The two items grant in aid (sub-head C) and appropriation in aid (sub-head K) need explanation. A grant in aid is 'moneys provided by Parliament,' but it differs greatly from an ordinary vote. As is shown in the footnote to the account, it is given once and for all, not for the year only. Unspent balances are not repaid, as we shall find that unspent balances of votes are, but can be used in the next or subsequent years. Unless specially subjected to audit (the above grant in aid is so subjected), it escapes the audit which other expenditure goes through. The receiver gives a bare receipt for it and has not to render an account. It is really a payment of a different character altogether, for grants in aid are given for objects Parliament wants to help and yet not to be responsible for. The grant in aid, for example, to the British Museum is for buying books, or other objects of historical or artistic interest: the Museum is given the money, and trusted to make the best use of it. Or a grant may be made to some poor Protectorate to enable it to balance its accounts.

Appropriations in aid (sub-head K) are revenue, received by the department, not paid into the Consolidated Fund, but retained and deducted off the gross sum of the vote. For example, the £33,439 estimated to be received by the British Museum is made up by sales of publications, of picture postcards, interest on invested benefactions, and special gifts from patrons of learning. Appropriations in aid were regularised by the Public Accounts and Charges Act, 1891. The Treasury is the authority which allows the appropriation. Departments are usually allowed to retain revenue as appropriations in aid if it is revenue which is germane to their business, and accrues at convenient times of the year.

Certain departments, such as the Land Registry and the Public Trustee, which are not officially revenue departments, now take in far more than they expend in performing their duties. Estimates for these and similar departments are, however, presented and passed, for an estimate is not only a sanction of expenditure, but also a sanction for the performance of certain functions. In such cases the sum asked for is a nominal one, and the vote is called a ' token vote.' In 1930 the Treasury decided that all ' token votes ' should be for the sum of £100.

The system of appropriations in aid has had curious results. First of all, it is a breach of the sound rule that all receipts should be paid into the Consolidated Fund, and that all payments should be made out of it. It is argued that this objection is met by the fact that appropriations in aid are not true revenue at all, that their inclusion would inflate the apparent revenue, that they are cross entries, and complicate book-keeping. But this is not so. Most of them, though small in amount, are true revenue ; and as for complication, it is a strange argument that if accounts are simple it does not matter if they are incomplete. No doubt the Treasury exercise a wise discretion in deciding what revenue a department should pay into the Consolidated Fund and what it should be allowed to keep : but why should it keep any ? It is said that if departments could not do so, if they could not thereby reduce the amounts for which they had to ask the House of Commons (a matter on which a departmental chief ponders night and day), they would be less active in collecting such revenue.

But this is untrue, and no one who has the slightest knowledge of the civil service would ever advance it. Another result of the system is that, by a ruling of the Speaker, a member may not move to reduce an appropriation in aid, presumably on the ground that thereby the net charge on the taxpayer would be increased, and also by reason of the wording of the Public Accounts and Charges Act, 1891, which gave the Treasury the duty of allowing appropriations in aid and by inference withdrew them from the committee.

At first sight, therefore, this ruling might appear to deprive the House of Commons of control over the gross total of any vote which contained appropriations in aid, though it can, and does, criticise the items for which that gross sum is provided. As, however, the gross total of a vote consists of Exchequer grant plus appropriations in aid, a reduction of the Exchequer grant, which is perfectly in order, reduces the gross total as effectually as would a motion to reduce appropriations in aid. Moreover, a department can never spend more than this gross sum, even though appropriations in aid produce more than was expected, and give it a bigger income.

The whole question of appropriations in aid was considered by the Public Accounts Committee of 1930, and interesting memoranda on the matter by the Treasury and the Comptroller and Auditor-General are included as appendices to their report. The Committee decided that there was no reason why the existing system should be altered.

The estimate printed on page 28 is a typical civil service estimate. The figures are set out plainly, but they are not in the form in which an accountant would cast them. A scientific analysis of expenditure is lacking. For in the larger estimates the votes and sub-heads do not record the total cost of any specific object of expenditure, but show the cost of a single item, such as pay, which is relevant to many services. The result is that it is almost impossible to calculate the true and complete cost of any particular service, an obvious handicap in criticising expense. Comparison is thereby made difficult. It should be possible, for example, to see at a glance the comparative cost of a man in the army and a man in the air force. That is a simple problem, but it becomes much more difficult when you have to correlate the cost of an inspector of schools under the Board of Education with that of a factory inspector under the Home Office, and almost insoluble when you try to relate the value of work done against staff employed in two diverse departments such as the Ministry of Pensions and that of Labour.

Departments in varying degrees do try to give costing figures of a sort, but these figures, at the best, are in a statement explanatory of the estimates and not bound up with them, and may be embodied in the annual report of the work of the department, where the figures cannot easily be disinterred. From 1919 to 1925 the army kept its accounts on an income and expenditure basis, but decided – and their decision was upheld by the Public Accounts Committee – that in the absence of decentralisation the application of the new system of account was impossible, but that cost accounting should be employed wherever applicable. There at the moment the matter rests, though no doubt a modern and unified system of accounting, by facilitating criticism, would strengthen the control of the House of Commons.

CHAPTER III

THE HOUSE OF COMMONS

In the last chapter the method whereby the executive arrived at the probable financial requirements for the year has been described. The estimates in which these requirements are embodied have been traced up to the time when they are presented to Parliament. The next step, or rather steps, rest with the legislature, for the executive has temporarily come to the end of its financial powers, since it cannot disburse one farthing until it has obtained parliamentary sanction for the expense, and been provided with the necessary funds by the same authority.

The somewhat tangled skein of financial procedure in the House of Commons will become easier to unravel if the following points are clearly understood :

1. That by standing order of the House of Commons no expenditure can be imposed and no tax levied except in committee of the whole House.

2. A committee of the whole House is really the House of Commons under another name. It is the House presided over, not by a robed and bewigged Speaker, raised above the clamour of parties in his chair of state, with the mace on the table in front of him, but by the chairman of committees or his deputy elected from amongst the government's supporters for the duration of a

Parliament, sitting alongside the clerks of the House at the aforesaid table, beneath which the mace has been placed out of sight. A member, too, on addressing the committee, must recollect to begin, not with the words "Mr. Speaker," but "Mr. Chairman," or he may even address him by name, and he must remember also to refer to the body he is addressing as "the committee" instead of "the House." These differences are picturesque and formal, but there are others which go rather deeper. The atmosphere of a committee of the whole House is freer and, to the new member, less terrifying. A member may speak to the question before the committee as often as he likes – or, rather, as often as the chairman will call him and the committee tolerate him – while in the House itself he may only speak once to each such question.

3. All resolutions passed by such committees are reported to the House and have to be agreed to by the House sitting as a House, with the Speaker in the chair. This means that all business discussed in committee of the House can also be discussed on report, a procedure which is often much criticised. It is true that nowadays the provision often leads to a tiresome reiteration of arguments already heard perhaps *ad nauseam* in committee. Historically the House, jealous of granting money to the executive, no doubt adopted a procedure which would give every opportunity for dissent to make itself heard, and even now the fact that financial business has to undergo the double process ensures that publicity is obtained for the proposed expenditure, and may even indirectly deter a government that is short of parliamentary time from putting forward proposals involving the expenditure of

public money. In practice, however, the committee or the report stage is frequently taken as purely formal business.

4. The committees of the whole House that have to deal with financial business are :

(*a*) The Committee of Supply ;

(*b*) The Committee of Ways and Means ;

(*c*) A committee of the whole House appointed for the consideration of a specific financial motion.

The Committee of Supply authorises the yearly expenditure by passing the estimates presented to it. The Committee of Ways and Means has, as its name implies, a double function. First, by authorising the issue from the Consolidated Fund of a sum equal in amount to the totals voted in Committee of Supply, it provides a way for the government to meet its expenditure. Incidentally, this procedure gives the House of Commons a dual control over the expenditure of the executive, for the Committee of Supply criticises all expenditure in detail and the Committee of Ways and Means can prevent the government making any expenditure at all.

The second function of the Committee of Ways and Means is to provide the Consolidated Fund with an income. So it is in this committee that the Chancellor opens his budget, and by its resolutions that taxes, or the means whereby the government is to pay its way, are first authorised. The following bills whose objects will presently be apparent are founded on resolutions passed by the Committee of Ways and Means : (1) Consolidated Fund Bills ; (2) Finance Bills ; (3) Appropriation Bills.

It has been stated (p. 26) that great policies such as that of de-rating, involving the Exchequer in the expenditure of millions of pounds, do not make their first appearance in an estimate, but in the terms of a bill authorising a department to carry out specified duties, and the Treasury to provide the necessary money either out of 'moneys provided by Parliament' or 'from the Consolidated Fund or the growing produce thereof.' By the standing order, no expenditure may be embarked on except in committee of the whole House. A motion, therefore, covering the proposed expenditure must first be considered by a committee of the whole House appointed for that purpose. If the proposition meets with the approval of the committee, the subsequent resolution is reported to the House and must be agreed to by that body before the clause authorising the expenditure can become embodied in the bill.

If the bill in question has for its main object the creation of the charge, the financial resolution must pass committee and be agreed to on report before the bill can be introduced. But if the charge is subsidiary only to the bill's main purpose, the bill can be introduced, printed, pass second reading, and be sent to a committee before the financial resolution is taken : but the clauses of the bill which create the charge are printed in italics, and cannot be considered by the committee to which the bill has been committed until the necessary financial resolution has passed through committee and been agreed to on report. The Speaker decides whether the charge is the main object of the bill or not. This is the procedure for both government bills and those promoted by private members[1] should any

[1] This distinction has an important practical result. Generally speaking, any member can bring in a bill on any subject, whereupon it is printed at public expense and circulated. But a bill whose main object is to create

such bills propose to impose a charge upon the people. The resolution authorising the charge must be put on the order paper by the Financial Secretary to the Treasury signifying that the proposal has the sanction of that department, and a Privy Councillor must signify the King's consent before the resolution is moved. The minister at the head of the department concerned usually explains the nature of the proposal and moves the resolution. In the same way, should a bill be introduced into the House of Lords containing provisions involving a charge (a course sometimes adopted owing to the congestion of business in the lower House), the financial clauses are left out of the bill by the Lords on third reading and have to be inserted by the Commons after the necessary resolution has been passed in a money committee.

Such committees are appointed from time to time during the session, vary in number each session, and usually, though not always, affect the finance of a future year. They are necessary to complete the mastery of the House of Commons over taxation and expenditure, but they lie rather outside the annual financial routine of the House of Commons, since the expenditure has only been authorised in general terms, and, if charged upon 'moneys provided by Parliament,' has to be implemented by a detailed estimate.

In theory, then, the mastery of the House of Commons over finance is complete, but the power

a charge cannot even be printed, unless the government move the financial resolution, which means adopting the bill, and this they hardly ever do. Consequently a private member can never get such a bill printed and its contents ventilated, e.g. a bill to lower the age at which old age pensions are granted. His only chance is to move a motion on a private member's day. But his right to move such motion depends upon his luck in the ballot, and, even if he gains the approval of the House, and a resolution to the required effect is passed, it cannot bind the executive.

of the government over the House, mentioned in the Introduction, must not be forgotten, as in practice it limits and, many critics say, vitiates the Commons' control of the purse.

The Committees of Supply and of Ways and Means, then, are the keystones of the annual financial procedure of the House of Commons, and are appointed by a resolution of the House, come to at the instance of a member of the government as soon as the opening business of the session, viz. the address in reply to the speech from the Throne, has been despatched. All estimates when presented are referred to the Committee of Supply. By another standing order which enshrines the most ancient of its privileges, namely the right of discussing grievances and having them remedied before considering supply, the House of Commons provides, on first[1] going into supply on the army, navy, air force and civil estimates, that amendments relating to the proposed estimates may be moved to the question that Mr. Speaker do now leave the chair. By this means ministers in charge of the service departments are afforded an opportunity of a general review of the work of their department, after which the first amendment on the order paper is called. As the civil and revenue estimates are not a homogeneous entity, the debate on Mr. Speaker leaving the chair on these estimates usually proceeds directly to the amendment which is to be discussed.

Private members ballot for the right to move

[1] This is a modern concession to enable the government to get through its business. Prior to 1882 the Speaker had to put a question on his leaving the chair whenever the order of the day for supply was read, and that motion was debatable. Now by standing order he leaves the chair without question put except on the four occasions specified.

some motion on this occasion, the subject of which must be germane to the estimates to be discussed. A wide latitude is given both in the choice of subject and in the subsequent debate. Only one such motion can be put to the vote, though, if time allows, other motions may be debated, but not voted on: and after the House has gone into committee, the estimate of which notice has been given is discussed.

The financial year ends on the 31st March; after that date the executive, without getting fresh authority from Parliament, is powerless to spend one farthing of the public money. It is, however, obviously impossible for the House of Commons to consider in detail and approve the whole expenditure for the year between February, when the estimates are usually presented, and the end of the financial year, while, if departments were forced to present their estimates earlier, close estimating would be even more difficult than it is now. In practice, consideration of the estimates goes on throughout the spring and summer, and by standing order need not be completed earlier than 5th August. So the gap between 1st April and that date when Parliament finally grants the supply must somehow be bridged if the work of government is to proceed. This is done in two ways. An estimate is presented for the civil and revenue departments for such a lump sum as will enable departments to carry on their work for four or five months. To this estimate is attached a schedule showing the amounts allotted to the different departments. This vote on account, as it is called, is submitted to the Committee of Supply early in March, and one day is allotted by standing order for its discussion in committee and another for the subsequent report of the committee to the House. Thus the expenditure for civil and revenue departments for the next three or four months is authorised by the passage of the vote on account through committee and report stages. About the same time the estimates for the three fighting services are presented, and the votes for men, pay, works, and one or two other big items in each of the three estimates are taken in Committee of Supply. The vote on account for the civil and revenue departments does not technically come within the definition of 'first going into supply,' and consequently the Speaker is not, as a rule, got out of the chair on these estimates until after 31st March, but he does have to go through this process three times before that date, as the army, navy and air force votes cannot be considered in Committee of Supply until the standing order has been complied with. The necessary votes once granted, and agreed to by the House on report, the fighting services are provided with sufficient money to carry on throughout the summer, for, unlike the civil and revenue departments, the navy, army and air force may temporarily use money voted for one purpose for something quite different, provided that the total of no vote is exceeded, and that Treasury sanction for such a change is obtained. Thus by about 20th March the House of Commons has sanctioned sufficient expenditure to keep the work of government going throughout the summer. Now comes in the function of the Committee of Ways and Means, which votes out of the Consolidated Fund a lump sum equal to the vote on account and the sum of the votes obtained for each of the three fighting services. On this resolution is founded the

Consolidated Fund Bill,[1] which, when it has received the royal assent, legalises the withdrawal of the sum mentioned above from the Consolidated Fund. The gap is bridged, and the government can afford to wait for more money until the House of Commons has examined the estimates at its leisure.

Twenty days, which, at the option of the government, may be increased to twenty-three, being days before the 5th August, are by standing order allotted to the business of supply. No day on which the question is put that the Speaker do leave the chair is included, but, on the other hand, two of the days are occupied by the discussion on the vote on account. An allotted day has to be devoted entirely to supply, and no other business may be taken before eleven o'clock in the evening of any such day. Provision is also made in the standing order for putting the question on all outstanding votes in committee on the last day but one of the allotted days, and all outstanding reports on the final day.

An estimate, like all expenditure, must be moved by a member of the government in committee of the whole House. That is an invariable rule. Consequently the estimate printed on p. 28 will be moved by the Financial Secretary to the Treasury in Committee of Supply. He either makes an explanatory statement, or merely formally moves and waits to see if any criticisms are offered by members. The debate then is open, and any member may speak, and speak as often as he can get the chairman to call him. It is informal; questions are asked and answered at once, and the speeches are short and unrhetorical. But on important

[1] A Consolidated Fund Act is not an Appropriation Act (*see* p. 52), for it authorises a lump sum only, not an individual sum against each vote.

estimates, such as those of the Ministry of Health or the Board of Education, the minister in charge makes a longer speech reviewing the whole government policy in connection with that specific service. Each vote is put separately from the chair, and, until the penultimate allotted day, can be debated and voted on separately. The chairman on the specimen estimate given will put the question, 'That a sum not exceeding £181,471 be granted to His Majesty to defray the charge which will come in course of payment during the year ending 31st March, 1932, for the salaries and other expenses of the British Museum, including a grant in aid.'

Once an estimate has been presented to the House of Commons, not even a member of the government can move to increase it. If he wants to do so, he must either present a supplementary estimate, or withdraw the original estimate and present a new one. Nor can he attach a condition to it or alter its destination, for that is, in effect, a fresh grant, and requires a fresh estimate. And, of course, a private member can do so still less. But either a member of the government or a private member can move to reduce it.

What can a private member do? Four things. He can speak or vote for the vote, or against it, or move to reduce it, or he can, in effect, take a vote that the vote be increased. True, no private member can ever *move* to impose or increase an expenditure or tax. But he can suggest to the government the desirability of increase, and can take a vote, in which such members of the committee as support him in the lobby do in fact vote for an increase. He does this by a parliamentary fiction. For instance, if he thinks that the Principal Librarian of the British Museum is paid too little, as very possibly he is, he can move the following motion : 'Civil Service Estimates, Class IV, Vote 2 : To reduce Sub-head A by £100.' Sub-head A, as he will see from the explanations which follow the estimate, includes the Principal Librarian's salary. If he wants it increased, he must move that the appropriate sub-head be reduced. His whole speech will urge an increase, and his vote and those of his supporters will be cast in favour of an increase.

The estimates put down for discussion on any supply day are, in practice, chosen by the opposition or oppositions, for, as only a selection of the year's expenditure can be reviewed in Committee of Supply, it is right that the critics of the executive, not the executive itself, should choose the subjects for discussion. Supply days can be put to various uses : grievances can be aired, great questions of policy debated, but economy in detail is rarely discussed, and still more rarely successfully discussed in a committee of six hundred. Departments who happen to be in the political limelight may have their estimates debated on several allotted days, with the result that on the last two days a vast amount of expenditure is passed without a word on it ever having been said. Obviously this system is not satisfactory, but as yet none better has been devised. A Select Committee appointed in 1931 to review Parliamentary procedure is understood to have turned its attention particularly to this problem, and all who are interested in Parliamentary institutions will hope that they may find a satisfactory solution.[1]

[1] Owing to the financial crisis of 1931 and its political reactions, the committee had no time to frame a report. The evidence taken before it is however published.

The proceedings in Committee of Ways and Means on granting a lump sum to cover all the supply votes, are nearly always purely formal. The estimate could be debated again at this stage, or on certain later stages of financial procedure ; but this rarely happens. The debate on it takes place in Committee of Supply, or on report.

For all resolutions passed by the Committees of Supply and Ways and Means, like the resolutions of any other committee, are reported to the House with the Speaker in the chair and the mace on the table. Here much the same process is gone through, and all questions can be debated again, but remember the rule stated before, that no expenditure can be authorised except in committee of the whole House. It can never be done on report. Any increase involves a new estimate in Committee of Supply. But an estimate can be reduced on report even on the motion of a private member, and of course it can be rejected.

It has been convenient to deal with the method of granting supply as a whole, but, in fact, it goes on throughout the summer and in point of time is interrupted by another financial process. The mechanism whereby the government secured its expenditure for four or five months, culminating in the Consolidated Fund (No. 1) Bill, has already been described. It is obvious, though, that the Consolidated Fund, if not fortified, would very quickly go bankrupt, as the income tax and surtax, on which it very largely relies, cease to have effect from 5th April. The Committee of Ways and Means, therefore, betakes itself to its second function, and in it the Chancellor of the Exchequer opens his budget, somewhere in the first half of

April. Expenditure which is the governing factor in the preparation of a budget is by that time pretty well known, for the estimates for the Supply Services have been presented, and the Consolidated Fund Services expenditure, which does not require annual parliamentary sanction, is a fairly constant figure.

This expenditure, sanction for which has been obtained once and for all, is for services which are charged not on 'moneys provided by Parliament,' but on 'the Consolidated Fund and the growing produce thereof.' Examples of such payments are the salaries of judges of the High Court, the King's civil list, and interest on the national debt. Consolidated Fund Services differ from services paid for out of annual votes not only in their more permanent character - some of the latter are in reality permanent - but in the fact that they are, whilst services charged on the votes are not, withdrawn from parliamentary criticism, once the act providing for them has been passed. This is often done advisedly: for were the salaries of all judges voted annually, every word spoken by every judge, from the Privy Council to the police court, could be criticised in Parliament - with results dreadful to contemplate.

The expenditure on these grants does not, however, vary greatly from year to year, for the House of Commons is naturally jealous of granting expenditure which will not come up annually for a fresh sanction, so that by the end of March a very good guess can be made at the revenue that the Chancellor will require. But, although estimates of expenditure are public property, those of revenue are not.

These estimates are obtained from the Board of Inland Revenue, the Board of Customs and

Excise, the Post Office, and the other income producing departments, but, unlike those of expenditure, are given to the Chancellor alone. Their secret is jealously guarded, and offers an interesting field for the ingenuity of amateur financiers. More especially, not a hint is allowed to escape about increase or remission of burdens, especially of customs or excise : for, if it were known that the sugar duty was to be reduced, importers would hold back supplies in order to get in at the lower rate : while the knowledge that sparkling wines would pay more would open veritable floodgates of champagne.[1] The finance of the year might be seriously compromised, speculation would be rife, and the consumer would gain no ultimate benefit. Although the forecasts of inland revenue and of customs and excise are estimates, they are wonderfully accurate. All factors which will increase income over that of last year -- good trade, good harvest, good weather and such-like -- have been allowed for, and so have the adverse features. The experts at inland revenue and customs may err here or there, but their totals are remarkably true. Often one error corrects another.

As ' Budget Day '[2] draws near, public excitement grows and the benches of the Chamber are usually packed when, the Speaker having left the chair, the Chairman of Ways and Means calls on the Chancellor of the Exchequer, and it is in rapt silence

[1] Twice in recent years withdrawals of tobacco from bond have been limited by Treasury order during the period immediately preceding the budget. In one case no increase was made in the rate of duty, in the other the rate was increased.

[2] This date cannot now be later than 4th May. The income tax year expires on 5th April. By the Provisional Collection of Taxes Act, 1913, the Ways and Means resolutions reimposing it must be passed within one month of 5th April, if they are to be operative immediately on passing. But see later (p. 50) as to the whole effect of this important act.

that he starts on the long business of opening his budget. By tradition, and to delay his announcement of remission or imposition of taxation until after the Stock Exchange has closed, the Chancellor starts his speech with a review of the finance of the year which has just closed, and gives the final balancing of that account. If there is a surplus, it goes by statute in reduction of the national debt. Surpluses paid over in this way are called the Old Sinking Fund. Any deficit will have been covered by borrowings. That matter cleared out of the way, he turns to an examination of the state of the national debt, with a general disquisition upon the condition of the country's finance, trade and prosperity. Next comes a forecast of revenue for the current year on the existing basis of taxation, and a comparison of it with expenditure, including any new expenditure, such as repayment of debt or fresh services, which the government may contemplate. If he anticipates a surplus in the coming year, he can use it to pay off debt, or to reduce taxation, or spend it on new services. If he anticipates a deficit, he must impose new taxes, or increase old ones, or borrow. Then – and this is where excitement quickens – he gives the details of such imposition, alteration or remission of taxation as circumstances may dictate or allow, and concludes with the final balance sheet.

Most taxes, being fixed permanently by statute, require no fresh legislation, unless the Chancellor seeks to increase or diminish the rate. It used, however, to be a well-settled practice that at least one important direct and one important indirect tax should be non-permanent, and reviewed by the House of Commons every year. Consequently income tax and tea duty were re-enacted annually. But since the tea duty was remitted in 1929, no indirect tax has now to be imposed afresh each year. So income tax and sur-tax and alterations of existing taxes are carried by resolutions which are often hotly debated. Private members can move reductions, though not increases, of a tax. If the government wish to drop an annual tax, all they have to do is to refrain from moving the resolution imposing it. Ways and Means Resolutions also specify the date when changes in taxation come into force. In addition to the specific tax resolutions, a general resolution is also passed, which enables amendments of previous Finance Acts, re-arrangements of debt, and other financial adjustments to be carried out, in the Finance Act which is to follow.

This, though not strictly necessary, is convenient, as the debate on such a general resolution can range over the whole financial policy of the government, and the opposition, therefore, have less objection to passing those resolutions dealing with the remission of existing or the imposition of fresh taxation, which must be voted by the Committee of Ways and Means before the changes of tax can become operative. The practice of allowing all resolutions save one to be voted on budget night, though of recent origin, is now well established. But the Ways and Means Resolutions have not in themselves the force of law ; they must be embodied in an Act of Parliament, a process, of course, which takes a considerable time. The old practice was to bridge the interval by collecting taxes at the rates authorised by these Resolutions, pending the passage of the annual Finance Act. In 1912, however, this practice was successfully challenged by Mr.

Gibson Bowles, who declined to pay income tax until it had been authorised by the Finance Act, and in so doing was upheld by the Courts. The dangers of allowing such a gap between the authorisation of the tax by the Committee of Ways and Means and the enforcement of its collection were patent. To meet them, the Provisional Collection of Taxes Act, 1913, was passed, which established the right of collection with certain qualifications, the most important of which are that the act only applies to customs and excise and income taxes, and to them only so far as relates to variations or renewals of taxes which were imposed in the previous financial year.

The Ways and Means Resolutions claim the benefit of the act, by including the words: 'And it is hereby declared that it is expedient in the public interest that this Resolution shall have statutory effect under the provisions of the Provisional Collection of Taxes Act, 1913.' As the act only gives the resolutions statutory effect for four months, it follows that its application to any resolution allows a total limit of four months within which the Finance Bill must be passed.[1]

[1] The act also provides that the resolutions to which it is applied must be agreed to on report within ten sitting days of their being passed in committee, and that the Finance Bill must be read a second time within twenty sitting days of the resolutions being reported. The act also ceases to operate if the provisions contained in the resolutions to which it has been applied are rejected, or if Parliament is dissolved or prorogued before the royal assent has been given to the Finance Bill. The effect of the Provisional Collection of Taxes Act, combined with that of the Parliament Act, is necessarily to curtail debate if the Finance Bill proves contentious. To take advantage of the Parliament Act, a bill must reach the House of Lords not less than one month before the end of the session. As the Finance Bill must become law within four months of the passing of any Ways and Means Resolution which seeks to take advantage of the Provisional Collection of Taxes Act, it follows that the House of Commons must agree to the resolutions on report and pass the Finance Bill through all its stages within three months from the date of the Chancellor opening his budget (assuming that all the resolutions except the 'amendment of the law' are agreed to on the first night).

This bill, which is the legal embodiment of the Ways and Means Resolutions, is ordered to be brought into the House of Commons as soon as that body has agreed to the last of the resolutions reported from the Committee of Ways and Means. It passes through all the usual stages – first reading, second reading, committee stage, report stage, and third reading. It is then sent up to the House of Lords, there to undergo a similar procedure. Finally it receives the royal assent and becomes law. The various stages of the bill in the House of Lords are usually only formal, though financial debates do take place there on the second reading. In the Commons it can be, and is, debated in all its stages, except that of first reading, which is formal. The main financial debates on principle take place on the last resolution in Committee of Ways and Means, on second and third readings, those in detail on the report stage of the resolutions, and on the committee and report stages of the bill. Many of these detailed provisions are extremely complicated, and to the layman almost unintelligible, especially those amendments of the law introduced at the instance of the revenue departments. Such amendments are necessary, because high taxation, like high pressure, finds out the weak places in the vessel, and, once a taxpayer has made a gap in the hedge, many are the sheep who are anxious to follow. It must impose no charges higher than those contained in the Ways and Means Resolutions.[1]

[1] Should the government wish to include in the Finance Bill taxing provisions not included in the Ways and Means Resolutions, they must introduce new resolutions in Committee of Ways and Means. Or, again, if any provision of the bill imposes a charge either on voted money or on the Consolidated Fund, as, for example, for debt redemption, a Financial (or Money) Resolution must be taken in committee of the whole House. The procedure is that described on p. 37. The clauses in the Finance Bill imposing these new charges are printed in italics.

Towards the end of the summer, then, the Finance Bill passes the House of Commons, and at about the same time the process of supply described on pp. 42–45 is coming to an end. When on the last allotted day but one the Committee of Supply has completed its work, the Committee of Ways and Means is asked to revert to its first function and to vote a resolution authorising the issue from the Consolidated Fund of a sum equal to the total voted for the civil and revenue departments, and for the navy, army, and air force departments, less the sums already included in the Consolidated Fund (No. 1) Bill (*vide* p. 42). On the last allotted supply day the House agrees to all the outstanding reports from the Committee of Supply and the report of the consequent resolution of the Committee of Ways and Means. The proceedings, both in Committee of Ways and Means and on the report of its resolution, are usually purely formal. After the report of the Ways and Means Resolution has been agreed to, the Consolidated Fund (Appropriation) Bill, which is founded on this resolution, is ordered to be introduced. This bill, which passes through all the usual stages, first authorises the issue from the Consolidated Fund of the total sum necessary to complete the money required for the Supply Services for the year, and allows the Treasury to borrow up to that sum in anticipation of revenue. It also limits the expenditure on each department to the sums set out in the schedule to the act, thereby completing the second great safeguard of the House of Commons against improper use of public money. The first is that the House can limit the total expenditure in any year, and the second that it can ensure that that expenditure is only incurred on specified subjects. The schedule in question reproduces Part I of each vote passed by the Committee of Supply since the passing of the last Appropriation Act, usually a year before, and it is the Speaker's duty to see that the various sums are entered correctly. The signification of the royal assent to this act marks a definite stage in the financial proceedings of the year, the main part of which has, by this act, been concluded.

It must, however, be borne in mind that departments are called upon in December to frame estimates for a period which only ends in the following March year. The surprising fact under these circumstances is not that departments are sometimes rather out in their estimates, but how close to the estimates their expenditure ultimately proves. If, however, a department does find, towards the end of the year, that its unspent balance is running perilously low, and obviously will not last out the year, it must come to the House of Commons with a supplementary estimate, which goes through the same processes as the original one. These supplementary estimates are naturally kept as low as possible, and anyone who has had some experience of wringing one out of the Treasury knows that it is far from pleasant to have to make such a demand. The Committee of Supply[1] considers these partly before Christmas and partly in the time between the meeting of the House after Christmas and the 31st March.[2] The issue of the sum necessary to cover

[1] The debates, however, are restricted to the necessity for the supplementary estimates themselves, and to points of policy thereby raised: and must not, as a rule, refer to the policy of the original estimate. But see Erskine May, pp. 536, 536 *n.* and 537 *n.*

[2] The guillotine of supply does not apply to supplementary estimates, which are, therefore, fair game to the member desirous of obstructing government business. Debates on very small sums are sometimes very prolonged – another reason for the Treasury's dislike of 'supplementaries.'

the total expenditure voted on supplementary estimates is, as a rule when there is no hurry, authorised by the same set of Ways and Means Resolutions and subsequent Consolidated Fund Bill as that in which the issue of the following year's vote on account (*see* p. 41) is authorised, and is appropriated in the Appropriation Bill of the ensuing summer.

But, with all its care, a department, at the end of the year, may find that its total vote has been exceeded. The sum in question is usually very small, but that, of course, makes no difference. As soon as the accounts have been audited and presented to Parliament (which is usually in the January following the 31st March on which the financial year in question comes to an end), the Treasury, on behalf of the sinning department, presents an excess estimate. This is first scrutinised by the Public Accounts Committee, and the accounting officer in question is examined. The committee have power to disallow the charge, and in that case the accounting officer would be personally responsible for the amount of the overspending. If, however, his explanations satisfy the committee, they report to that effect to the House. The excess vote is then passed by the Committee of Supply, and also goes into the first set of Ways and Means Resolutions and the subsequent Consolidated Fund Bill, in this case being voted nearly a year after the close of the financial year to which it relates. But even this, late as it is, is not the end of the long story. As has already been described, the three fighting services, unlike the civil and revenue departments, have power, subject to Treasury sanction, to transfer savings on one vote to counterbalance over-spendings on another, provided the grand total of the vote for the service is not exceeded. These transfers, however, require parliamentary sanction, so when the appropriation accounts for these services have been presented to Parliament in January of the year following that to which the accounts relate, they are examined by the Public Accounts Committee, and, if no fault is found in them there, a resolution is passed by the House to set up a special committee of the whole House to consider navy, army and air force expenditure, and the requisite appropriation accounts are referred to that committee. When a resolution agreeing to the transfers is passed and agreed to on report,[1] the necessary legal authority is given in the schedule to the next Appropriation Act, usually that passed fifteen months after the close of the financial year to which these transfers relate.

One other method of granting money is open to the House of Commons. It is only employed if a sudden emergency, such as a threat of war, should require special and immediate expenditure. A vote of credit is introduced in Committee of Supply. It grants a lump sum to the government, not allocated to any particular service. It passes Committee of Supply and of Ways and Means, and is then either included in the next Consolidated Fund Bill or in a special Consolidated Fund Bill of its own. Like other votes, it is available only for the year, and a balance unspent must be surrendered.

Before closing the chapter it may be convenient to sum up the financial procedure of the House of Commons by a skeleton outline, with examples

[1] The proceedings both in committee and on report are usually purely formal, the detailed examination having been made by the Public Accounts Committee.

taken from an actual session. The session 1929–30 opened on 25th June, 1929. The financial business for the year ending 31st March, 1930, had already been dealt with in the previous session.

1. The Committees of Supply and Ways and Means were set up at the conclusion of the address, on 10th July.
2. Estimates of expenditure for the year ending 31st March, 1931 (in future called the year 1930), were presented to the House and referred to the Committee of Supply on 25th February, 1930. (In an emergency the government would have presented a vote of credit, which is an estimate without any details.)
3. The civil service vote on account was passed by the Committee of Supply on 4th March and agreed to on report on the 10th March.
4. The Speaker was got out of the chair on the navy estimates on 17th March, on the air estimates on 18th March, and on the army estimates on 24th March, and on each of these days substantial votes for each of the services concerned were obtained. All these votes were reported and agreed to on 25th March.
5. The corresponding Ways and Means Resolutions were passed in committee on 24th March, and reported and agreed to on 25th March, on which day the Consolidated Fund Bill was introduced. It received the royal assent on 28th March.

The government's expenditure for three or four months of the ensuing financial year was now provided for.

6. The Speaker was got out of the chair on the civil and revenue estimates on 31st March.
7. The budget was opened in Committee of Ways and Means on 14th April, all the resolutions except the Amendment of Law being agreed to on that evening. The last resolution was agreed to on 10th April. The resolutions were reported on 30th April, and the Finance Bill introduced on 6th May. The bill was passed by the House of Commons on 25th July, receiving the royal assent on 1st August, the day on which Parliament was prorogued.
8. Between 17th March, which was the first allotted day, and 24th July, the House devoted eighteen days to the business of supply.
9. The nineteenth allotted supply day was on 29th July, and the twentieth on 30th July. On the nineteenth day all outstanding estimates were voted in Committee of Supply and the corresponding Ways and Means Resolutions in that committee. On the twentieth day the report stage of all Supply and Ways and Means was taken, and, on the latter being agreed to, the Appropriation Bill was introduced. This bill passed the House of Commons on 1st August, and received the royal assent on the same day, the day on which Parliament was prorogued.

This concluded the main financial business of the year. Parliament reassembled on 28th October, the address was agreed to, and the Committees of Supply and Ways and Means set up on 4th November, but the Speaker did not again have to be got out of the chair, as the business for the same financial year was being dealt with.

10. A supplementary estimate was presented on 14th November and considered on 9th December. As the money for this service (Exchequer contribution to Unemployment Insurance) was urgently required, the corresponding Ways and Means Resolution was passed on the same day, both resolutions were agreed to on report on 11th December, and the consequent Consolidated Fund Bill received the royal assent on 19th December.
11. Further supplementary estimates were presented on 12th December and 16th and 26th February, 1931. They were considered in committee on 16th December and on five separate days in February. Their corresponding Ways and Means Resolution was passed in committee on 24th March, and the subsequent Consolidated Fund Bill received the royal assent on 27th March.

That concluded the finance of the year 1930 until after the accounts for that year had been audited. Meanwhile the accounts for the year ending 31st March, 1930 (the year 1929), had been audited, and it was found that three civil departments and the navy had over-spent their votes.

A. Excess votes accordingly were required, and these were presented on 20th and 24th February, considered and passed by the Public Accounts Committee, considered in Committee of Supply and agreed to on 3rd and

18th March, the necessary Ways and Means Resolution being passed in committee on 24th March, and subsequent Consolidated Fund Bill received the royal assent on 27th March.

It will be noted that the Ways and Means Resolutions of 24th March and the consequent Consolidated Fund Bill (which also dealt with the vote on account for the year 1931) dealt with the finance of the years 1929, 1930 and 1931.

B. On 17th July, 1931, the House resolved that on Tuesday next it would resolve itself into a committee to consider army and air expenditure for 1929, and the appropriation accounts for 1929 were referred to the committee. On 21st July, accordingly, the committee approved of the transfers made between various votes in the two departments concerned (the navy had had their transfers authorised at the same time as they had got their Excess vote sanctioned). Thus items 10 and 11 referring to the year 1930 and items A and B referring to the year 1929 were all included in the Appropriation Act, which received the royal assent on 31st July, 1931, an act which dealt of course mainly with the Appropriation of Supply for the year 1931.

CHAPTER IV

COLLECTION OF REVENUE

THE legislature has, in the processes which have been described in the last chapter, authorised both expenditure and the method of meeting that expenditure, namely taxation. It then becomes the business of the executive to collect and spend the money which Parliament has granted. The money is spent in the performance of the multifarious duties of government. The pay, food and clothing of the fighting services, the grants made to local authorities for housing, for health and for educational services, and the wages of the servants of the state and the cost of the buildings in which they work, all form part of the national expenditure. Anyone who studies, however hastily, a volume of the civil estimates, will be amazed at the number and variety of the tasks performed by a modern government. To meet this expenditure the nation has an income derived from four sources: taxes, the yield of certain national assets, fees for services rendered, and borrowing. The last, a dubious form of income, must be used when the receipts from the first three are insufficient to cover expenditure, or when liabilities fall due before cash wherewith to meet them is collected. It will be dealt with later; at present we are concerned with the three other sources of income.

This chapter will show how the revenue from

them is collected, and how it is made available for spending.

For the most part the revenue is paid into a central fund known as the Consolidated Fund or the Exchequer Account, though there are certain receipts which are used where they come to hand and never reach the central fund at all.

Of the three forms of income, taxation is by far the most important. In 1914 it represented 82 per cent., and in 1930 90 per cent., of the total national revenue. Before going on, however, to describe the manner in which taxes are collected, a word must be said of the two other sources of revenue. The income-yielding assets of the state are the Crown lands and certain investments, such as shares in the Anglo-Persian Oil Company and in the Suez Canal. Dividends from these shares are paid directly into the Consolidated Fund. On the other hand, the Commissioners of Crown Lands collect the rents arising from the properties and pay over the proceeds. But it is net revenue which they so pay over. Like any other landlord, the state has certain expenses in connection with the upkeep of its estates. These are not voted by Parliament, in the way of other public expenditure, but are paid out of the revenue arising from the estates ; and it is the revenue remaining after these expenses have been paid which goes into the Consolidated Fund. Here, then, is the first exception to the principle that this fund should represent total receipts. It is not in itself important, as the sums which thereby escape parliamentary control are not considerable. But the principle is of vital importance, and all exceptions are, for that reason, to be deprecated.

Of the fees received by departments, the receipts of the Post Office are the largest, so large, in fact, that the Post Office is classed as one of the revenue departments. The procedure adopted by all these three departments in dealing with their receipts is the same, and will be described when the methods of the strictly tax-collecting departments are examined. Many other departments collect minor sums during the course of their work. Some of them pay these receipts directly into the Consolidated Fund. But others (and these now form the majority) treat their receipts as appropriations in aid. In this way a double transfer of money is avoided, the receipts are paid into the Paymaster-General's cash account, where they are placed to the credit of the service concerned, and the departments draw a proportionately smaller sum from the Exchequer for their voted expenditure. This is an administrative convenience, but an important contravention of the idea of the Consolidated Fund. The possible dangers of appropriations in aid have already been pointed out, but so long as the House of Commons has to sanction the service, and the total amount of the appropriations in aid that may be used, the system does not seem to represent a serious danger to Parliament's control over finance.

All these sources of revenue, however, are trifles compared with taxation. The House of Commons imposes the taxes : the two great revenue departments extract the money from the pocket of the taxpayer, and transfer it to the Consolidated Fund. The Board of Inland Revenue collects direct taxes, the principal items of which are income tax, surtax and estate duty ; while the collection of indirect taxes is the province of the Board of Customs and Excise. Put briefly, the duties of these two departments consist of assessment, prevention, collection and transfer. The revenue departments can also give the Chancellor of the Exchequer valuable information, when he is considering the imposition of new, or the alteration of old, taxes. The cost and difficulty of collection, as well as the probable yield of any tax, are obviously vital considerations, and on these points the revenue departments alone are in a position to offer expert advice.

The manner in which indirect taxes are collected may first be considered. The primary problem which faces the Commissioners of Customs and Excise is to ascertain the amount of goods liable to duty. In the case of excise, this means the amount of dutiable goods or services produced, and in the case of customs, the amount of such goods entering the country. Closely allied with this problem is that further one of preventing the evasion of duty. A large staff of excise officers is employed, to keep account of the dutiable goods produced, and to see that no such goods escape taxation. The country is divided into areas, and these again into districts, each of which is in charge of a surveyor, and under the surveyor are stations controlled by officers. Each officer is responsible in his district or station for supervising, not only the production (and in coastal stations the importation) of dutiable goods, but also entertainments, licences and other activities liable to excise.

In the case of customs this supervision entails the examination of every ship reaching this country, and the control of her cargo. When a ship arrives at the quay she is boarded by customs officers, who rummage to see that no dutiable goods are concealed about her. None of her cargo may be delivered from the quay until the importer has obtained papers known as 'entries' from the custom-house. Before claiming delivery, therefore, the importer must attend the custom-house with a list of the goods which he is importing. These goods may be free, or subject to duty. If they are free, the importer obtains an 'entry' signed by custom-house officials, which he presents at the quayside. The goods are examined by an officer to see that the importer's declaration is correct, and, if all is in order, the goods are delivered to him. If, on the other hand, he is importing dutiable goods, three courses are open to him. He may wish for immediate delivery, or he may trans-ship the goods for re-export, or he may wish to store them for a time. In the first case he pays duty forthwith, and, having done so, obtains an 'entry' which enables him to remove the goods from the quay. Goods for re-export are not subject to duty, and, in the case of such transactions, the importer gets an 'entry' from the custom-house which enables him to trans-ship the goods, and the process is supervised by customs officers. If – and this is the third alternative – the importer does not wish for immediate delivery of the goods, there is an arrangement whereby he can store them in a bonded warehouse. He makes no immediate payment, but enters into a bond with the government for the amount of the duty. The goods are then removed from the quay, under the supervision of customs officers, and stored in the bonded warehouse. These warehouses must be approved by the Commissioners of Customs and Excise. They are furnished with a Crown lock and key, and are under the supervision of a customs officer. No goods may be released from them without his authority. The importer houses his goods in the warehouse until such time as he wishes to re-export them or to dispose of them for consumption in this country. In the former case no duty is payable, and the goods are removed to the port under bond, and this bond is finally discharged by the customs officer's certificate of shipment. In the latter case duty must be paid, and the importer discharges his bond, and obtains delivery of his goods by payment to the custom-house.

Thus the custom-house maintains a strict check on all goods entering the country, by a system of examination and control. In the case of excise, supervision entails a great variety of procedure. The officer has to keep watch over excise licences and entertainment duties, as well as over dutiable goods produced under very various conditions. It is easy to measure quantities and check evasion where goods are manufactured on a large scale. This, for example, is the case with spirits. Beer, on the other hand, may be produced on a large or on a small scale. A description of the control exercised over beer gives a good illustration of the system. It must be noted, however, that procedure varies in each instance, according to the conditions of production.

Before a brewer can make beer for sale he must take out an excise licence, and must fill in a form describing in detail his premises, and the vessels to be used in production. In this way all brewers are known to the department, for, though beer can be brewed on a small scale, illicit production is easily detected. Breweries are visited by officers a number of times during the week, and at the larger breweries an officer is permanently stationed. The brewer must give notice to the officer whenever a brewing is to take place, and he must record in a book (known as his brewing-book) the quantity and nature of the materials used at each brewing. The officer knows the amount of beer which should be produced from a given quantity of raw materials, so that from the entries in the brewing-book he can calculate what is called 'the theoretic quantity' of beer produced. This theoretic quantity is a check on the actual quantity declared by the brewer. When the brewing reaches a certain stage the liquor is run into fermenting vessels. These are gauged, so that the quantity contained in the vessels is very accurately known. The brewer measures the quantity contained in the fermenting vessels, and ascertains the gravity of the liquor, both of which figures he enters in the brewing-book. The officer, who has had notice of the brewing, may then come and take his own measures and check the entry made by the brewer. Officers do not always inspect each brewing, but the brewer must leave the liquor in the fermenting vessels for twelve hours, in order to give the officer an opportunity for inspection. The bulk quantity produced at each brewing, in conjunction with the gravity, shows the standard quantity on which duty must be paid. The officer compares his estimate of the standard quantity with that of the brewer and with the theoretic quantity calculated from the raw materials, and duty is charged on whichever amount is the largest.[1] In this way the officer is

[1] With a 6 per cent. allowance for waste.

able to exercise a very complete check over the quantity of beer produced. If he has reason to suppose that the brewer is evading his control, he has very considerable powers of inspection and search.

By this system of supervision, the surveyors are able to prevent the entry into consumption of goods which have not paid duty, and to ascertain the amount liable to duty. They have then to make an assessment, after which there remains the question of collection. This is the function of the collector, who is the head officer in each area. The surveyors who work under him furnish him with reports of their assessments, which they also communicate to the head office. The total of the assessments in his area is a charge against the collector who is responsible for the collection of this amount. It is his duty to receive the money which is paid over to him by the assessed persons. He pays the money which he receives into his official account at the local bank, and every day he makes remittances from thence to the cash account of the Commissioners of Customs and Excise at the Bank of England. He then notifies the Accountant and Comptroller-General, who is the head of the financial department of the Board of Customs and Excise, of the amount remitted, and forwards to him the branch bank receipt for the transfer. It should be added, though more will be said about it later, that for current expenses the collector keeps back a certain amount of cash in hand and of credit at the local bank. Every day he furnishes the Accountant and Comptroller-General with a statement of receipts and payments. The statement of his remittances is compared with the passbook of the Board's general account, which is made up daily by the Bank of England. That is the check on the bank. What about the check on the collectors? As we have seen, it is the duty of the surveyors to furnish the head office with a report of the amount of goods liable for duty which are produced and imported into their area. From these reports the Accountant and Comptroller-General can ascertain the amount of duty which should have been collected and paid in. This amount is compared with the receipts shown in the accounts of the collectors, and an independent check is thus established on the amounts received and paid in by them.

So much for prevention, assessment and collection. The money is safely lodged in the Bank of England. We must now witness its transfer to the Consolidated Fund and the manner in which the expenses of collection are met. Every day the Accountant and Comptroller-General transfers money in even thousands from the general account of the Commissioners to the Consolidated Fund at the Bank of England. He does not remit the whole balance, however, but keeps back a certain sum for replenishing his drawing account, which is a balance for the payment of current expenses. Now the expenses of revenue departments have been voted by the House of Commons in the same manner as other Supply Services, and to ensure the control of the House they must be paid out of the Consolidated Fund. The principle is maintained, but by a roundabout procedure. In order to avoid unnecessary transfers of money, the revenue departments draw upon their receipts for the payment of these expenses, and moneys so used are treated as advances on account of the vote. The expenditure incurred by the department is met provisionally out of the balances retained by the collectors at their local banks, and by the head office in its drawing account. Once a month a statement is sent to the Treasury of the sums thus borrowed from revenue on the vote account, and the Treasury then authorises the transfer of this amount from the Consolidated Fund to the general account of the Commissioners at the Bank of England. Thence, on the same day, the Commissioners return it to the Consolidated Fund, thus paying back to revenue the amount that has been borrowed for expenditure.

The Board of Inland Revenue treat departmental expenditure in the same way. They, too, draw money from their general account to pay for vote expenditure, and the money is periodically repaid by the Treasury. Let us now see how they collect our taxes. Surtax and estate duties are administered centrally, income tax locally. As the latter forms so large a part of the revenue received by the Board, it is as well to study its collection in detail. Here, as in the case of excise, the Board is met with the problems of assessment of tax, prevention of evasion, and, finally, of collection. In outline, the system adopted is as follows. A form is issued to the taxpayer on which he must make a return of income. These returns form the basis of assessment. A careful enquiry is made into their accuracy, and they are examined and checked as far as possible. But such an enquiry is inevitably difficult, because in many cases the taxpayer alone is in possession of complete information. There is an effective check in the case of incomes of salaried persons, through the returns of salaries made by the employer, and a partial check in the case of limited liability profits through the accounts which companies furnish, but at present the production of full accounts for purposes of assessment can only be enforced in cases of appeal. With the small trader who does not keep accounts, and the professional man in the receipt of fees, an adequate check on the return is almost impossible. One course, however, is open to the assessing authority, when it is thought that a return underestimates income. The taxpayer can be assessed on a higher income than he has returned, and the onus of proof is then shifted on to his shoulders. If he is able to bring evidence in support of his lower figure, he can appeal against the assessment, otherwise he accepts the estimate made. There is a further safeguard against the inaccuracies of the individual's return to which much importance is attached. This is the system of deduction at the source. Limited liability companies are assessed on the full amount of their profits before the payment of any dividends, and on distributing dividends to their shareholders they are entitled to deduct the appropriate tax from the amount paid. As the profits of limited liability companies are more easily checked than the incomes of individuals (the publication of accounts is compulsory in the case of public companies), this system greatly facilitates assessment, and the great bulk of income tax is collected in this way.

The assessment having been made, notice is sent to the collector and to the taxpayer. At this point the taxpayer may make an appeal against the assessment, and, if the matter cannot be settled by negotiation, the case is heard by the Commissioners, of whom more hereafter. The collectors[1] then proceed to collect the amounts due and to pay them into their local banks. As in the case of excise revenue, the total of the assessments made in his area is a charge against the collector, and he is responsible for the collection of this sum. His receipts are checked by the assessments. The collector may not draw on the account at the local bank. At stated periods the bank manager transmits the moneys collected to the Board's account at the Bank of England. Thence daily transfers are made to the Consolidated Fund, but as in the case of customs, the whole amount is not transferred; a balance is retained for the payment of expenses and to meet claims for repayments and rebates.

This is the scheme of income tax collection in outline. In practice the system is complicated by the fact that there are two authorities concerned. In each division of the country, unpaid local authorities are appointed, known as Commissioners of Income Tax, who are independent of the Board of Inland Revenue. It was originally intended that these commissioners should be responsible for the administration of the tax. But, side by side with this voluntary body, there is in each district an inspector of taxes, appointed by the Board of Inland Revenue. He is assisted by a staff of clerks. In theory, his duty is not to administer the tax, but to observe its administration by the commissioners in order to safeguard the interests of the state. The commissioners appoint an assessor (who is not a whole time government servant, but is in

[1] The collector until 1931 was in most cases the officer of the district commissioners, not of the inland revenue. In 1931 the Public Accounts Committee recommended that, for the better safeguarding of the revenue, all collectors should be appointed by the Board of Inland Revenue. A provision to that effect was enacted in the Finance Act of the same year.

receipt of fees), and, according to the strict law, it is he who issues forms, examines the returns of taxpayers, and makes the assessment which is then allowed by the commissioners. It is to this body, also, that appeals against assessment may be made. This system was established at a time when the administration of the tax was much less complicated than it is at present. The difficulties of assessment have now become so considerable, the examination of returns and the settlement of liabilities so technical, that a voluntary body is no longer able to deal with them adequately. Consequently a great deal of the work has now devolved upon the inspector. He, who was originally an observer, has become chief actor. In practice it is he who checks the returns, examines accounts, and ascertains the liability of the taxpayer. Notices of appeal are sent to him, he makes the necessary investigations, and in a large number of cases is able to settle the matter with the taxpayer, without anything more than the formal consent of the commissioners. They, however, still hear appeals, which is their most important duty. The Royal Commission on the Income Tax urged very strongly that this anomalous arrangement should be abolished. They recommended that the work of commissioners should be confined to the hearing of appeals, and that the business of assessment should be by law, as it is in fact, the duty of the inspector. There is little doubt that they were right, and it is to be hoped that the existing makeshift arrangement will be replaced by a more orderly and modern system.

Enough has now been said to show the manner in which the revenue departments perform their duties. Taxes are imposed by the House of Commons, and it is the province of the revenue departments to see that the money arising from these taxes reaches the Exchequer with the least cost to the state and the least inconvenience to the taxpayer. They must not let money slip through their fingers in the process, and, as we have seen, assessments once made, adequate checks are provided against loss in transfer. The receipts of the collectors are checked by the returns of the assessors, and the banks are checked by the returns of the collectors, while the expenses of the departments are confined to the amounts voted by Parliament. These expenses are paid out of revenue in the first instance, but this process involves a debt which must be repaid to the Consolidated Fund. The revenue departments cannot escape the control of Parliament by spending more from revenue than has been allotted them. What they have spent must be repaid, and should they exceed their allowance they must go to Parliament in the guise of debtors to ask for a supplementary estimate. In the end, therefore, the total revenue collected finds its way into the Consolidated Fund. It is the process of assessment which is the danger-point in the whole system. This is the gap by which revenue may evade the tax-collector, and, as will be evident from the foregoing description, it is round the question of assessment that the problems and difficulties of the revenue departments centre. The rest may be considered a matter of routine, but this is a problem involving judgment and responsibility. The departments have to steer a middle course between two evils. On the one hand, they must not work their system in such a way as to cause undue inconvenience or irritation to the taxpayer, and, on the other hand, they must not be so lax in their investigations as to let incomes or commodities escape taxation. It does not lie wholly with the departments, however, to make the system of assessment as watertight as possible. It depends partly on the legal powers given them, and partly on the nature of the tax imposed. When the taxes imposed are such as to tempt or to facilitate evasion, the difficulties of the departments are increased. High rates of income tax make evasion tempting, and excise duties levied on a number of goods produced in small quantities make it easy. The Royal Commission on Income Tax made certain recommendations which would undoubtedly facilitate the investigations of the inspector of taxes. They suggested that the assessing authority should have power to require the production of full accounts certified by the taxpayer, and they recommended that the penalties for incorrect returns should be made more severe. It is difficult to understand how these reforms would damage any but the fraudulent.

The tax-collector is, however, not greatly beloved by his fellow-citizens, and so far Parliament has been reluctant to give him wider powers, even though thereby his revenue-collecting efficiency would be greatly increased. It is, however, now time to turn from the tax-collector and his victim and probe somewhat more deeply into the workings of that central fund into which the revenue has been seen flowing in a very steady stream.

CHAPTER V

THE CONSOLIDATED FUND

THE Exchequer or the Consolidated Fund (it can be called either) is an account at the Bank of England. Into this account is paid the money collected by the revenue departments, the income which the state receives from its various properties, and any money which the Treasury may have raised by borrowing. The fund therefore represents national receipts, and in this and the succeeding chapters the machinery which governs the spending of this income will be considered. The present chapter deals more particularly with the restraints which protect the fund from misuse, or at least from uses not sanctioned by the House of Commons.

Three principles underlie the idea of a Consolidated Fund.

First, all the receipts of the state should be paid into a single fund, and all expenses of the state should be paid out of it. This is a principle of good accountancy, and it is also of paramount importance in facilitating central control.

Secondly, the fund, which represents the total income of the state, should be under the control of Parliament and not of the government. Parliament's ultimate hold over the executive lies in its power to refuse money. In order to exercise this power, Parliament must be in a position to stop all issues from the Consolidated Fund.

Thirdly, issues from the Consolidated Fund should be made, not only with the sanction of Parliament, but also only for purposes approved by Parliament. This is allied to the second principle, but with a difference : the former means that the government may be forced to resign by the refusal of Ways and Means, whereas this third principle means that, even when Ways and Means have been granted, they can only be spent on purposes approved by Parliament, which means, in fact, the House of Commons : for the rights of the Crown have lapsed, and those of the House of Lords practically so.

How far does the actual system conform to these excellent principles ? To the first there are some exceptions. The receipts which accrue to certain spending departments in the course of their work are treated, with the sanction of the Treasury, as appropriations in aid,[1] and are paid by the departments which receive them, not into the Consolidated Fund at all, but into the Paymaster-General's cash account. The expenses of the revenue departments are paid in the first instance from revenue, some of which is withheld from the Consolidated Fund for the purpose ; but, as we have seen, accounts are made up every month, and total revenue is then paid into the Consolidated Fund. Thus this is no real breach of the principle. It does not weaken the House of Commons' control over expenditure. The same cannot be said, however, with regard to appropriations in aid. It is clear that these are an important, and might become a serious, exception to the principle that total income

[1] Appropriations in aid up to the limit voted by the House of Commons are paid into the Paymaster-General's account. Sums beyond that limit are paid into the Exchequer.

should be paid into the Consolidated Fund, and all expenditure disbursed from it.

Other exceptions are of a different character from those just mentioned. The Road Fund was established under the Roads Act, 1920, to finance road development generally. It had allocated to it as income the whole of the proceeds of the taxes on mechanically propelled vehicles imposed by the Finance Act, 1920. These taxes are collected by local authorities and by them paid into the Exchequer, which, in turn (subject to a relatively small deduction), is bound to pay them into the Road Fund Account.

Two consequences which are conducive neither to economy nor to equity of taxation spring from the special assignment of these taxes. First, then, the total proceeds must be spent on the maintenance of roads, although a more profitable use might have been found for the money. This is an uneconomic procedure, for it is obvious that, if money is spent on a less urgent service while the needs of the more urgent remain unsatisfied, the maximum benefit has not been obtained from expenditure. Indeed, the result may be excessive and wasteful expenditure on roads. Secondly, the persons who pay the taxes are in a position to demand that the rate imposed should be fixed by the amount that is needed for the purpose for which the tax was raised. Thus an artificial limit is placed upon the money that can be raised by a tax, which is in effect a luxury tax, and which might otherwise prove a profitable source of revenue.

But although, theoretically, the principle of taxation specifically allocated to a particular service had little to recommend it, it was only a period of acute financial stringency that broke down the privileged position of the Road Fund and enabled the general taxpayer to obtain some relief from the productivity of the taxes on mechanically propelled vehicles. In 1926, the Finance Act authorised the payment of seven million pounds sterling to the Exchequer by the Road Fund, whose future income, moreover, was reduced by one-third. In the following year the Finance Act provided for a further raid on the balance of the fund, and a further sum of twelve million pounds sterling was swept into the Exchequer. It would, however, probably have been more satisfactory to return at once to the ordinary method and finance road development by vote in the ordinary way. The result of leaving the fund with a reduced income and a diminished balance was to bankrupt it and force it to meet its commitments by borrowing. As a result of the financial crisis of the autumn of 1931, the deficiency on the year's working of the fund was met out of moneys provided by Parliament and voted in Committee of Supply.

The year 1920 also saw the initiation of another fund which has had an unfortunate history. The Unemployment Insurance Fund was set up with an income consisting of contributions from employers, employees and the state, and with a liability to pay unemployment benefit at certain fixed rates. The Treasury was empowered, under the original act, to maintain the solvency of the fund, but this proved an impossible task, and by the autumn of 1931 the debt of the fund had reached the figure of one hundred and fifteen million pounds sterling. In the financial crisis of that autumn the question of balancing the Unemployment Insurance Fund loomed large, and an estimate to provide for the presumed deficit was presented in September. As the deficits on both the Road and the Unemployment Insurance Fund are now being met out of moneys provided by Parliament, it would seem that the moment has arrived to abolish both the funds and provide the money by a vote in supply, of course using any receipts as appropriations in aid.

The other two principles deal with Parliament's power over the executive through its control of the Consolidated Fund. It is worth while looking at the actual machinery to see how this control is exercised and how complete it really is.

The department which administers the Consolidated Fund is the Exchequer and Audit Department. The head of this department is the Comptroller and Auditor-General. The peculiar importance of his office is reflected in his status. He is responsible to no minister, but is the servant of the House of Commons alone. His function is to keep watch over the expenditure of governments through his control of the Consolidated Fund. He is specially appointed by letters patent, and is removable only on a joint address of both Houses of Parliament, an event which can hardly ever happen. His salary, like that of a judge, is not included in the annual estimates, but is a charge on the Consolidated Fund. In this way his independence of governments is secured. By means of his control over the Consolidated Fund, he holds the key to the national income, and when governments want to spend money, they must come to him to unlock the doors of their treasure-house.

The system adopted by the Comptroller in

issuing money for Supply Services differs from that for Consolidated Fund Services.

The money for the latter services is not voted annually, nor is it voted to the Crown, but there is a standing authority from Parliament for its payment. At the beginning of each quarter a requisition is sent by the Treasury to the Comptroller and Auditor-General, demanding money for Consolidated Fund Services. The requisition gives a list of the charges for which the money is required. The Comptroller and Auditor-General goes through the statement in detail to see that there is authority for each payment. He carefully checks the requisition of the Treasury, and makes no issue unless he is assured that the payment is a duly authorised charge on the Consolidated Fund. When he is satisfied that all is in order, he grants the credit to the Treasury and informs the Bank of England. The Treasury can then draw upon the Consolidated Fund up to the amount and for the purposes stated. It does not make the payments direct from the fund, but transfers money for meeting debt charges to the Bank of England, which is responsible for making such payments, and money for meeting other charges it transfers to the account of the Paymaster-General. This account, like the Consolidated Fund, is kept at the Bank of England, and therefore the money never leaves the bank. During the course of the quarter further requisitions will be presented, examined in the same way by the Comptroller and Auditor-General, and at the close a schedule of the total charges during the quarter is sent in. The Comptroller scrutinises the schedule, assures himself that all the charges are in order, and when he is satisfied, issues the balance.

Over Consolidated Fund Services, therefore, the control of the Exchequer and Audit Department is complete. The Comptroller and Auditor-General checks each issue that is made and sees that the sums demanded are authorised charges on the fund. The government can only obtain credits up to the amount due, for the Comptroller and Auditor-General is in a position to limit them to this amount.

The issue of money for Supply Services is somewhat different. This, it will be recollected, is expenditure authorised afresh each year by the House of Commons, and, in examining the financial machinery of the legislature, it was shown that before any grant of supply is valid a corresponding Ways and Means Resolution, embodied in a Consolidated Fund Act, is required authorising the issue of a lump sum from the Consolidated Fund. The vote in supply is technically a grant to the Crown, and, until the Treasury obtains the sovereign's authority, they cannot make free with his money. The first step, therefore, is to get a royal order,[1] and that the Treasury proceeds to do. This is not such a formidable procedure as it sounds, and is now purely formal, since, in effect, the Treasury directs itself to authorise the Bank of England to pay over to the Treasury the money specified in the grant (which is recited). Armed with this authority, the Treasury writes to the Comptroller requiring him to grant them credits on the Consolidated Fund.

Consider the position on any 1st April, when the

[1] The royal order can be issued as soon as a vote has been passed in committee and agreed to on report, without waiting for a Ways and Means Resolution or a Consolidated Fund Bill, *provided that* there is still enough of the money previously granted for that same year left in the Exchequer to cover the issue which the new royal order seeks to authorise.

financial year begins. In March the House of Commons will have passed the Vote on Account, and this will have been perfected by the Consolidated Fund Act. The vote on account contains a schedule which sets out the sum which departments (except the three fighting services, which have a different system) require to enable them to carry on for the next four or five months: that is, until the Appropriation Act is passed, which finally grants their money. The Consolidated Fund Act authorises the Comptroller and Auditor-General to issue money from the Consolidated Fund up to the total of the sums in the schedule to the Vote on Account, and of the money voted for the other services. Note that the Consolidated Fund Act authorises issue of a lump sum, not, as does an Appropriation Act, a specified sum for each service.

Now, when the Treasury writes to the Comptroller and Auditor-General asking him to release money from the Consolidated Fund so that the departments can pay their bills, they do not ask, and he does not grant, the total amount included in the Consolidated Fund Act: that would mean that he lost control altogether of four or five months' expenditure, and that so far as he was concerned the Treasury might spend that money as they liked. No. He places at their disposal about a month's supply. His authority for granting the credit is of course the Consolidated Fund Act, and he must verify this act, and compare the amount of his grant with the total grant of the act. He then authorises the Bank of England to give credits to the Treasury on the Consolidated Fund, up to the amount which he has granted. This sum is now at the disposal of the Treasury, and though in actual fact it remains in the Consolidated Fund, the power to draw it out has passed from the hands of the Comptroller and Auditor-General to those of the Treasury. They draw upon the sum as money is required, authorising the Bank to make transfers from it to the account of the Paymaster-General. As will be seen in the next chapter, transfers to the Paymaster-General are made in respect of specified services, and the Comptroller receives daily from the Treasury an account of the total sum, and of the amount for each service so transferred. In this way he can see how much has been issued to the Paymaster-General on behalf of each vote. Total issues are also checked by the passbook of the Exchequer Account (the Consolidated Fund), which is made up by the Bank and forwarded daily to the Comptroller.

It will be seen that the credit granted to the Treasury is a lump sum, for it is not issued by the Comptroller in respect of specified services, but for supply in general. He has a check against misapplication. The Treasury render him an account of transfers to the Paymaster-General, and as these are for specified services, he can see that no vote is over-spent by comparing it with the schedule to the vote on account, and with the amounts voted for the navy, army and air force services. But this is a check after the event. How then do these facts accord with the principles stated above? And how far is the Consolidated Fund protected?

The Comptroller, by his hold over issues from the Consolidated Fund, can prevent the government getting money until it has been granted by a Consolidated Fund Act or by an Appropriation Act. He can prevent the government from securing a greater sum than has been granted, by ensuring that total issues do not exceed the total granted. But as the issues which he makes are unappropriated, he cannot directly prevent a government from spending money in ways other than those agreed upon by Parliament.

And this is the case with issues under Appropriation Acts as well as with those under Consolidated Fund Acts. It will be recollected that the Appropriation Act, passed late in the summer, is the final authority for the issue of the year's supply. It allots to each Supply Service the exact sum it requires, and authorises its issue from the Consolidated Fund. But here again the issues which the Comptroller authorises are not specific ; he grants to the Treasury a lump sum, not money for an individual service. Therefore a check against misapplication of money issued for Supply Services must be sought for elsewhere. Three other authorities are concerned in the matter. First, the Treasury, on which lies the responsibility of not transferring to the Paymaster-General more than the individual vote authorises. Secondly, the Accounting Officer of each department, whose duty it is to ensure that the expenditure of his department is confined to the amount voted ; and, thirdly, the Paymaster-General, who is also responsible for seeing that the expenditure on each service does not exceed the amount granted for that service.

Here, then, we have three independent checks against misapplication of money issued from the Consolidated Fund. These three authorities are all concerned to prevent unauthorised expenditure. And then, finally, there is audit. Audit is another and most important function of the Comptroller and Auditor-General, and it will be dealt with in a separate chapter ; for the present it is enough to say that the knowledge that audit is to come, and that misappropriation will be brought to light, is a powerful preventive against unauthorised expenditure.

That is the extent to which the Consolidated Fund is protected from misuse. Remember always that, unlike other financial functions, it is not in the hands of the government, but of the Comptroller and Auditor-General, who is an independent officer. He is in a position to check completely issues made for Consolidated Fund Services, and no more can be spent on such services than is due and authorised. For Supply Services he is not in such a strong position. As Auditor, he can censure misapplication of money, but as Comptroller he cannot prevent it. For the correct appropriation of public money, therefore, Parliament must rely on the activities of the Treasury, the Paymaster-General and the Accounting Officers. If these checks prove insufficient, the irregularity will be shown up in the Comptroller and Auditor-General's report, and the fear of this report is likely to make the other checks more effective. Moreover, should the unexpected happen, should governments act wrongfully and persuade the Treasury, the Paymaster-General and the Accounting Officers to abet them, it is impossible that the Comptroller and Auditor-General should not know, as he receives each day from the Treasury a schedule of payments made by the Exchequer to the Paymaster-General on account of certain specified votes. If the Comptroller became aware that misappropriation was taking place, he could at once report to the Speaker, and, if the case arose, doubtless would do so. The existing safeguards, therefore, completely prevent the government from getting hold of any more money from the Consolidated Fund than it has been granted, and practically prevent it from spending that money otherwise than was intended. These restraints on the executive have been of enormous importance in the past. At present the danger is less that the executive shall act, and consequently spend, without the approval of Parliament, than that it shall obtain Parliament's consent to unwise expenditure. But this does not mean that the safeguards are superfluous. The knowledge that they are there, and that they can be made effective, is in itself a sufficient check. And should a government ever be put in office which desired to spend without the authority of Parliament, the importance of these regulations would again become apparent.

CHAPTER VI

THE PAYMASTER-GENERAL

WHEN money is issued from the Consolidated Fund by the Treasury, it is paid over either to the Bank of England for the service of the national debt, or else into the account of the Paymaster-General. The spending departments pay no bills themselves ; indeed, they have no banking accounts except those for the small sums necessary for petty cash expenditure in provincial offices. It is the Paymaster-General who pays the creditors of the state. Before reviewing his functions, it is well to recall that the titular Paymaster-General is a minor minister and a member of the government, but unpaid and doing no work in connection with his office. His work is done for him by the Assistant Paymaster-General, a civil servant and head of the Pay Office. It is to this officer that the title Paymaster-General will in the course of this chapter be applied. He and his office are not under their nominal political chief, but under the Treasury.

The Paymaster-General cannot himself affect the amount or the nature of expenditure. His concern is with two functions only :

First, to make the payments for which the state has become liable, and to see that these payments are made to the correct person with the minimum of risk, delay and machinery.

And, secondly, to ensure that the expenditure

on any service does not exceed the amount granted by Parliament for that service.

There are two steps in the process of paying the state's creditors, first the identification of the claimant and the establishment of his claim, and secondly the transfer of money. The Pay Office has erected a system of checks to ensure that these two steps are fraught with as little risk as possible. With regard to the first point, the Paymaster-General must be satisfied that the liability has actually been incurred by the spending department, and that the individual making the claim is really the person to whom payment is due. The spending departments give their creditors drafts on the Pay Office, and send daily to the Paymaster-General a schedule of authority, which tells him what drafts are issued, their amounts, and the persons to whom they are payable. It is signed by two officers of the department, and the staff of the Pay Office must verify the signatures. Cheques or money are not sent by post. The draft is presented for payment either by the creditor or by his bank, is compared with the authority received from the spending department, and, if all is in order, payment is made. The manner in which money is actually transferred is as follows. Small amounts may be paid in cash, and the Paymaster-General draws from his drawing account a small balance for this purpose. In such cases the creditor calls for his money at the Pay Office, and verification of the draft, its signature by the creditor and payment over the counter, complete the process of transfer. The majority of payments, however, are not made in cash, and in these other cases the creditor pays the draft into his bank and the banks attend daily at the Pay

Office with the drafts which have been paid in by their various customers. Each bank adds up the amounts due on the drafts which it holds for presentation, and claims the total sum from the Pay Office. The drafts are then verified, and, if they are found correct, the Paymaster-General writes off the total amount due to each bank from his account at the Bank of England, where, by a book entry, it is transferred to the account which the bank keeps there. For purposes of accounting and audit the receipted drafts are either kept by the Paymaster-General (as in the case of pensions) or returned to the spending departments. Here the Paymaster-General's function ends ; it remains to the various banks to credit those customers who have paid in drafts with the respective amounts obtained from the Pay Office.

This system appears to provide adequate checks on the payment of public money, and, when the payee has a banking account, is not unduly cumbersome. When, however, he wishes to be paid in cash, he has to attend at the Pay Office in person or else to send an agent. In the case of some departments, cash for weekly salaries and establishment charges are collected by the department's cashier from the Paymaster-General, and are paid over by him to the officers concerned. There are also a number of local paymasters who are responsible for expenditure which has to be made out of London in cash, such as payments to soldiers and sailors and the like. The Paymaster-General, acting on a draft from the department concerned, issues money to these local paymasters, which they then hold on imprest and for which they are responsible.

That is the machinery whereby Supply Services are paid. The Paymaster-General has to make two other classes of payments, those for Consolidated Fund Services and those for non-effective payments. He does not make payments on the national debt, for this is done by the Bank of England. Other Consolidated Fund Services he pays according to a quarterly schedule issued by the Treasury.

Non-effective payments include both war gratuities and war pensions, now very large, and also civil and pre-war pensions and gratuities. A different system is adopted in the two cases. In the case of war pensions, the Paymaster-General receives from the Ministry of Pensions a list containing the names of pensioners, amounts of pensions and period for which they are granted. That is his authority, and it is a continuing authority for the period of the pension. On receipt he writes to the pensioner, sending him a form of application to fill up and asking whether he wants to be paid in cash or by bank draft. On getting this back, the Paymaster-General sends him the appropriate forms for receiving the pension. Pensioners are paid monthly or quarterly, as the pensioner chooses. If the pension is for less than a year, he sends forms covering the whole period : if for a year or more, forms for the year. On or after the date of payment, but not before, the pensioner fills in and signs the form, which includes a declaration of his identity and also of course proves that he is still alive, and then either pays the draft into his bank or calls at the Pay Office, presents it there and gets the cash. Further forms are sent him as required. It will be seen that the responsibility for issuing the warrants, for paying the right person, and for satisfying himself that the pensioner is still living, rests on the Paymaster-General. All that the Ministry of Pensions does is to tell the Paymaster-General that a certain person is entitled to a certain pension for a certain period or for his life. He does the rest.

In the case of other gratuities, and pensions, such as civil service pensions, he is actually the Accounting Officer, and all the responsibility rests on him.

But the Paymaster-General has other responsibilities, and his duty is not fully done if he contents himself with honouring the drafts made on him by departments. He must also see that the department concerned has a credit to its account, and that no department is ever overdrawn. To ensure this the Paymaster-General enlists the help of the Treasury, which, whenever it is granted a credit on the Consolidated Fund, communicates to the Pay Office a list of the total sums authorised by Parliament, and of the amounts appropriated to each service. Every day the Paymaster-General, taking his liabilities and his bank balance into consideration, sends to the Treasury an estimate of the sum which he is likely to need from the Consolidated Fund, for the payments of that day. The money is then transferred by order of the Treasury to the account of the Pay Office at the Bank of England, and the Paymaster-General is informed of the amount issued in respect of each service. He himself keeps accounts for the various votes, and enters the amounts issued from the Consolidated Fund and the amounts paid by him in respect of each vote. The vote, it will be recalled, is the unit of financial procedure. In this way he is able to ensure that no payments are made on behalf of any department in excess of the amount granted by Parliament.

The above, however, is a simplified account of what is in reality a rather complicated process, for it must be noted that while the Paymaster-General keeps separate accounts, he does not hold separate balances at the Bank of England in respect of each vote. The amount issued from the Consolidated Fund is allotted to specified services, but the whole sum is paid into a single account at the Bank of England, known as the Exchequer Credit Account.[1] Similarly, sums received in the way of revenue by the spending departments, as appropriations in aid (described in Chapter III), are paid into a single account at the Bank, which is called the Paymaster-General's Cash Account. These two balances at the Bank, the Cash Account and the Exchequer credit account, form the Paymaster-General's total supply of credit. He treats them as a general cash balance, on which he draws for all payments,[2] irrespective of the service to which they belong. This means that at a given moment he may have paid out in respect of one vote more than has been issued from the Consolidated Fund on behalf of that vote. Obviously this position could not be allowed to continue for long, or by the end of the year the Paymaster-General might find that, though total expenditure had not exceeded the total granted, the money spent on some particular service had been in excess of the sum authorised by Parliament. Such a transfer of credit from one vote to another is not permitted except in the case of the fighting services votes. It will be remembered that

[1] An alternative name for this account is the Paymaster-General's Supply Account.

[2] Payments are not made directly from these two accounts, but money is transferred from these, as required, to two working accounts kept by the Paymaster-General at the Bank of England. These two working accounts are known as the Drawing Account and the Bill Account.

the temporary needs of these services are not met from the Vote on Account, but they are given two or three of their big votes, and allowed to use this money for any authorised purpose, adjusting their accounts at the end of the year. Permanent transfers from one vote to another must, as has been explained on p. 54, be authorised first by the Treasury and finally by the House of Commons.

Consequently every month the Paymaster-General balances the vote accounts. If more has been spent on any civil or revenue vote than has been issued under that heading from the Consolidated Fund the Paymaster-General asks for a further issue on its account, so that at the end of the month sums expended correspond closely with the sum issued for each service. In the case of navy and air force votes the accounts need not exactly balance month by month, but a quarterly reckoning is made, and at these times the sums issued for all services closely correspond to the sums expended on each. At the end of the financial year a final reckoning is taken, and the net expenditure on each vote must be completely covered by issues from the Consolidated Fund on its behalf.

By balancing the vote accounts the Paymaster-General limits expenditure on each service to the amount voted by Parliament. At the same time, by keeping a single undifferentiated fund (represented by the balances on his cash account and his Exchequer credit account), he is able to work with smaller balances than would be practicable if he kept different bank accounts for each vote. For whereas with a number of balances he would need to keep on each a margin for unexpected liabilities, with a single fund uncertainties are likely to cancel each other in such a way that the total of a single balance may safely be lower than the aggregate of many smaller balances. This is important because the security of public money is increased by keeping outstanding balances at a low figure. A further advantage which ensues from this practice will be clear when it is remembered that payments into the Consolidated Fund are not a steady flow, but are made at irregular intervals. If the money in the fund at any moment is insufficient to meet the necessary outgoings, the government must borrow to fill the gap between expenditure and receipts. Unduly high balances in the hands of the Paymaster-General might necessitate borrowing, which might have been avoided had he worked on a narrower margin.

In addition to issues from the Exchequer and appropriations in aid, certain other balances are held by the Paymaster-General, and promote that economy of balances which has already been noted as so desirable. For the Paymaster-General, though of course keeping separate accounts of these moneys, includes them in the general balance of his Cash Account, where they form part of his total supply of money from which he meets all expenditure as it falls due. In fact, he uses up all the balance of his Cash Account before applying to the Treasury for money from the Consolidated Fund. These other balances held by the Paymaster-General are Deposit Funds, the Civil Contingencies Fund, and the Treasury Chest Fund.

Deposit Funds are moneys which come into the possession of various departments in the course of large transactions. They are sums held on deposit or suspense account, and are not due immediately or at all to the Consolidated Fund. Interest is not payable on them, and in most cases there is no legal direction to invest them. A part of them, however, is usually invested at the discretion of the Treasury. Part remains as cash in the Paymaster-General's cash account and is used by him to meet current expenditure.

The Treasury Chest is a small fund used for dealings in foreign exchange. No permanent payments are made from it, and it is kept at a fixed amount year by year. Various departments have to make payments abroad. The War Office, for instance, must pay its soldiers wherever they are stationed, the Foreign Office must pay embassy staffs, and the Office of Works must pay contractors. But the money granted to these departments is in England. Somehow it has to be transferred, and if the payment is to be made in some other currency, the pounds must be converted. In either case the question of exchange arises, and there is a possibility of loss or gain on the transaction. Now the sums voted by Parliament do not allow for fluctuating exchanges, and in fact the departments are not called upon to bear the risk. They do not go into the market and buy exchange as they require it, but for payments in a foreign country they draw upon the Treasury Chest Officer stationed there. These officers hold balances on imprest in a foreign country, where they serve as local paymasters. Drafts are drawn upon them by the various departments and are met by the Treasury Chest Officers in the local currency, as drafts are met in pounds by the Paymaster-General at Whitehall. When their balances need replenishing, they draw upon the Paymaster-General by means of a bill, or a telegraphic transfer. By discounting this bill at their bank, or by drawing on the credit created there by the telegraphic transfer, they obtain money in the foreign country and the Paymaster-General pays the bill in pounds when it is presented to him in London. Any exchange loss on the transaction is temporarily met out of the Treasury Chest Fund ; any gain goes to swell the balance of that fund in the hands of the Paymaster-General. At the end of the year the account is balanced, gains and losses are added up, and the Treasury Chest Fund is made up to the fixed amount. Any loss on the year is made good by Parliament voting the deficiency ; any gain is paid into the Consolidated Fund. In this way the departments are able to make payments abroad without the risk of buying exchange.[1]

The Civil Contingencies Fund is used for making small loans to the civil departments in anticipation of parliamentary grants. It is kept, like the Treasury Chest, at a fixed amount, and no payments are permanently made out of it. It is administered by the Treasury. Advances are made from the fund when there is urgent need for expenditure of a small amount, which has not been voted by Parliament. This may occur if the occasion arises for some small service which has not been included in an estimate, or if payments must immediately be made on behalf of a service which has not yet been voted by Parliament. Advances may also be made from the fund, if the Treasury agree that the overspending of a vote by a small sum is inevitable. The

[1] But a department's losses are not wholly paid for out of this fund. Part of them are borne on the votes. Thus in 1929 the depreciation of the Shanghai dollar led to heavy losses on Civil Estimates, Class II, Vote 2 (sub-head Y), leading to an excess vote, and on the Navy Vote II (sub-head O), *vide* Appropriation Accounts, 1929.

sums advanced from the fund must all be repaid eventually out of moneys provided by Parliament. In this way the fund is kept up to a fixed sum year by year, and the Treasury is provided with a small loan fund which it can use in emergencies. Its use may sometimes be a breach of the sound principle that no money can be paid unless the House of Commons has voted it : but there must be some means of meeting unexpected and extraordinary requirements, and so long as only small sums are paid out, as is the case with advances from the Civil Contingencies Fund, no danger is incurred.[1]

[1] In 1931 an estimate was presented for repayment to the fund for, amongst other things, the fees due on certain royal warrants, the expenses of the memorial service to Earl Balfour, the cost of a presentation to the Icelandic Althing, and the rebate of duty on certain foreign diplomatic cars. The total vote was for £35,127 16*s*. 5*d*. *Vide* paper H.C. 123 of Session 1930–31.

CHAPTER VII

AUDIT AND BALANCE

THE financial processes of receiving and spending have now been described. The national income has been collected and paid into the Consolidated Fund by the revenue departments. Money has been released from that fund by the Comptroller and Auditor-General, made over to the Paymaster-General by the Treasury, and by him paid over to the nation's creditors at the request of the departments concerned. There is a further piece of accountancy which must now be mentioned. At the end of the year the nation's accounts, like those of an ordinary business, must be balanced in order that the exact position of the national finances may be ascertained. The two principal accounts which show national expenditure for the year are the Finance Accounts and the Appropriation Accounts. The former are issued about the end of the summer, immediately following the end of the financial year, and show, for the year, the total receipts into, and issues out of, the Consolidated Fund, together with the amount carried forward to the next year. By comparing that sum with the amount brought in at the beginning of the year, the difference between receipts and expenditure can be ascertained.

If there is any surplus of revenue receipts over the expenditure on Supply and Consolidated Fund Services, that surplus is allocated to an account until some three months after the close of the financial year to which they relate, and, owing to the amount of work involved in their preparation and audit, they are not presented to Parliament until the following February or March. They record the total expenditure chargeable to the grant of the year, and this includes all payments, the orders for which were signed before the 1st April. All liabilities must be met in the year in which they fall due, and departments must not postpone the payment of sums due in order to charge expenditure to the grant of the following year. If the order for payment is signed by 31st March, the payment is included in the accounts of the financial year then ending, although it may not be actually met by the Paymaster-General until the succeeding year. That will depend on the date at which the payee presents his draft at the Pay Office. If he fails to do this within three months after the close of the financial year, a new draft has to be issued and the payment is charged on the vote, and entered in the Appropriation Accounts of the following year. Thus it is not until three months after the financial year ends that the departments know the total expenditure which has actually been paid out on their behalf, and not till then can the Appropriation Accounts be made up. These accounts show the whole expenditure which has been made during the year ; but, because drafts dated in one financial year may not be paid until the next, this total does not exactly correspond with the total issues made from the Consolidated Fund and recorded, as has already been explained, in the Finance Accounts for the year. The departments, therefore, cannot finally make up their Appropriation Accounts until the end of June, and before they can be published they have to be submitted to audit. For, just as an ordinary business customarily appoints an auditor to examine its accounts, so does the state. The purpose of any audit is to establish the correctness of individual entries and to see that the accounts, as a whole, present a true and complete statement of the financial business. This duty is entrusted by the state to the Exchequer and Audit Department, at whose head is the Comptroller and Auditor-General. The independent position of this official and his work as Comptroller have already been noted. His work as Auditor-General is far more important. By the Exchequer and Audit Act of 1866 the Comptroller and Auditor-General is required, on behalf of the House of Commons, to examine the accounts of the issues made during the year for Consolidated Fund and Supply Services, and to audit such other accounts as the Treasury may direct.

After his examination he has to certify the accounts as correct and to report to Parliament on his audit. In his examination the Auditor must ascertain first whether the payments shown in the accounts are supported by proofs of payment, and, secondly, whether the money expended on each service has been applied to the purpose for which the grant was intended to provide. In addition, therefore, to the check on book-keeping which is required of the ordinary commercial auditor, the Comptroller and Auditor-General must see that the expenditure on each service conforms to the schedule appended to the Appropriation Act, and that the payments made on account of each service are due and relevant thereto. He must also see that, in cases where Treasury sanction for any expenditure is necessary, such sanction has been obtained. (This is the case, for instance, with alterations in establishment charges, or the transfer of expenditure from one sub-head to another.) He is further required to examine the receipts of the spending departments and to see that they are put to the uses intended by the House of Commons.

In addition to accounts of expenditure, the Comptroller and Auditor-General audits the accounts of receipts of revenue. These accounts are not certified by him, for he cannot himself inspect the actual assessments ; but he must ascertain that adequate regulations and procedure have been framed to secure an effective check on the assessment, collection and proper allocation of revenue, and that any such regulations and procedure are being duly carried out by the department concerned. He also examines, as he thinks fit, the correctness of the sums brought into the Consolidated Fund, and reports the results of any such examinations to the House of Commons. In order to fulfil these various duties the Auditor must have full and complete access to all accounts and to the documentary evidence available. To this end, the accounts of the various departments are sent periodically to him, together with the actual vouchers supporting the charges. It will be remembered that the Paymaster-General returns the receipted drafts – known as vouchers – to the departments, and these, therefore, are submitted as proof of the payments having been made.

The Comptroller and Auditor-General verifies the statements made in the accounts, comparing them with the vouchers and receipts. In all doubtful cases, he questions the departments concerned and obtains additional information from the Accounting Officers. He goes very carefully into the question of appropriation, seeing that the expenditure on each service is in accordance with the intention of Parliament. Unlike a commercial auditor, he does not check cash balances in the keeping of departments. It has been ruled by the Treasury that this is not his province. This is a serious qualification of the Auditor's power to detect fraud, and, indeed, it is hardly considered to be his function to do so. It has been said of the commercial auditor that 'he is a watchdog but not a bloodhound,' and this is even more the case with the government auditor : the responsibility for such detection must lie to a large extent in the hands of the departments themselves. In dealing with revenue accounts, the Auditor sends officers at intervals to visit customs and excise stations, in order to check the accounts on the spot, and to see that the amount shown in the documents is duly collected.

The task of examining and checking the whole of the national accounts in detail would be a tremendous and costly undertaking. In practice the Auditor does not cover the whole field. In the case of certain departments he makes what is known as a test audit ; that is to say, he selects some point or section of the account and submits it to the closest possible detailed examination. For the rest of the account he satisfies himself that money in the mass is applied as Parliament has directed, and that the department concerned has duly examined the account and checked the vouchers. The departments themselves do not know what section of their accounts will be tested, and the Auditor makes his selection in such a way as to cover the whole field in a number of years. Before 1921 the system of a test audit was only applied to the accounts of the army and navy, but the Exchequer and Audit Act, 1921, enabled the Comptroller and Auditor-General to extend the system to the civil departments, at his discretion. In addition to his examination at headquarters, he carries out occasional test audits on the local expenditure of departments, for which purpose he sends down officers to conduct examinations on the spot.

The smaller departments submit their accounts, together with the vouchers and other evidence, once a month. In the larger departments the Comptroller and Auditor-General keeps a resident staff, who work on the department's own books. Thus, in both cases, audit is a continuous process carried on throughout the course of the year.[1]

The Comptroller and Auditor-General notes down any irregularities which the departments are unable to justify, and they go into his report at the end of the year. That may be a long way off, and an occasion might arise when it would seem advisable that the House of Commons should be acquainted immediately with some matter that had come to his notice. In that case he could go directly to the Speaker and get the matter laid before the House of Commons. Such an occasion has not actually arisen, but the fact that this course of action is open to him might prove of great importance.

Finally, at the end of the year the Accounting Officers of the various departments render their

[1] Of a staff of 230, 190 are quartered in the premises of the various departments.

Appropriation Accounts, made up by votes according to the schedule attached to the Appropriation Act, which, it may be remembered, contains the sums voted for Supply Services and the money appropriated to pay them (Part I of the estimate). They show, by sub-heads, the grants made and the actual expenditure and the actual and estimated receipts in parallel columns. The Appropriation Accounts are accompanied by a statement explaining the disposal of balances, and, in cases where the grant for any sub-head differs greatly from the actual expenditure, by an explanation from the Accounting Officer of the cause of the divergence.

In the case of the civil departments these accounts have to be rendered to the Comptroller and Auditor-General on or before 30th November following the financial year to which they apply, which ends, of course, on 31st March. Navy, army and air force accounts have to be rendered on or before 31st December. The Comptroller and Auditor-General examines them and sees that they agree with the periodic accounts submitted to him, and finally certifies them as correct, with or without reservations. He then forwards them to the Treasury, together with his report, and the Treasury must lay accounts and report before the House of Commons early in the following year.[1]

The report of the Auditor deals with the result of his examination. He draws attention in it to all cases where it appears to him that grants have been exceeded, or that money received by a

[1] The various dates laid down in the Exchequer and Audit Departments Act, 1921, are as follows :

	From Auditor-General to Treasury.	*Treasury to Parliament.*
Fighting services.	Not later than 31st Jan.	Not later than 15th March.
Civil and revenue.	Not later than 15th Jan.	Not later than 31st Jan.

department from sources other than the grants has not been applied or accounted for according to the directions of Parliament. He reports on any case which has come to his notice where expenditure has not been supported by Treasury sanction, and must consequently be regarded as not properly chargeable to the grant. He draws attention to any sum charged against a grant which he has found to be unsupported by proof of payment.[1] As a result, since the present system of audit was established in 1866, the accountancy of departments has become infinitely more efficient, and Accounting Officers more zealous in guarding against misappropriations.

But this is not all. So far two aspects of audit only have been considered : verification of the accounts, and verification of appropriation : appropriation, of course, being the application of money to the objects ordered by the House of Commons. But there is a third aspect which has tended recently to become of increasing importance. The commercial auditor is not concerned to see whether the business is being conducted prudently or imprudently : his duty is to ascertain and state the financial result of what has been done. On the Comptroller and Auditor-General, Parliament, by statute, has imposed somewhat similar duties, but successive Comptrollers have interpreted their instructions as including the examination and criticism of the nature as well as the regularity of expenditure. Successive Public Accounts Committees have supported them in this

[1] A brief summary of the scope of the Auditor-General's examination, and the lines on which he proceeds, is to be found in the Report of the Comptroller and Auditor-General on the Civil Appropriation Accounts, 1929.

attitude, which was formally recognised by the Select Committees on National Expenditure of 1902–3 and 1918. This is an interesting and an important development. The safeguards in our financial system offer, as we have seen, a fairly complete assurance that public expenditure is confined to the limits laid down by the House of Commons: what is particularly lacking is an assurance that the money granted by the House is well spent. In this matter the criticisms of the Auditor are undoubtedly of value. He is an outside and an independent examiner, and is in a position to bring to the notice of the House expenditure which appears to him unnecessary or ill-advised. But the power of the Auditor must not be overstated. It is sometimes possible for him to detect a glaring case of waste, but it is much harder for him to determine whether money spent has been laid out to the best advantage. Even the first point is difficult, since his data are confined to the accounts, the documentary evidence and what the departments choose to tell him. In many cases the departments themselves are alone in a position to know whether and how far money had to be spent. It is impossible for an outsider, coming in after the event, to have a full or competent knowledge of the conditions prevailing in each case, and the scope of his judgment is consequently limited. But the question whether money has been wisely spent is far more difficult, and one in which supervision over departments would be most valuable if it were practicable. The Auditor, however, has no means of knowing, and it is not considered to be his business to know, how much any object ought to cost. The most he can do is to observe if the cost of similar things is markedly different on different occasions, or in different departments. He can criticise, therefore, from the point of view of inconsistency rather than from that of excessive payment. Consistent extravagance might consequently go undetected, and deplorable as this may appear, it is difficult to see how any standard could be found of what payments should, and what payments should not, be considered excessive. In competitive enterprise there is a rough-and-ready test of efficient spending which is not available in government undertakings. The business man must sell his goods with a margin for profit if he is to continue in business. Consequently the amount which he spends on their production is conditioned by the amount which people are willing to pay for them. He may indeed spend unwisely, his costs of production may be unduly high, and he may not get the best value for his outlay. But his uneconomic spending will be reflected in his profits, and in the long run he will be ousted by more efficient competitors. The measuring-rod of profit is not available in the case of government expenditure. There is no competitor to oust the uneconomic department or to serve as a measure of its efficiency. Even comparison between the expenditure of various departments is difficult, because it is hard to find comparable units of cost. This is partly due to intrinsic differences in the nature of the services, and partly to the way in which the accounts are rendered. Accounts at present are not made up in such a way as to show the total cost of any object of expenditure. That cost is scattered under various headings, and it is impossible to isolate an item and to determine how much of the total expenditure was relevant to it.

With a view to obtaining more information on costs, and to facilitate comparisons, the Select Committee on National Expenditure advocated the adoption of cost accounting. The army accounts for some years were made up on this principle, so that the whole expenditure was analysed and it was possible to see the total cost of any section. This scheme, after very careful consideration, was found to be unworkable under the existing system of army administration and for that reason was abandoned.[1] But though the system adopted by the army proved unworkable unless accompanied by a complete reorganisation of the system of military administration, it is undoubtedly true that, unless accounts are comparable, it is nearly impossible to measure the efficiency of diverse departments. So it is possible that a unified system will have to be evolved. And there must be something more. Take as an illustration the clerical work carried on in many rooms, in many buildings in Whitehall. This work is largely the same, whether done in the Admiralty or in the Office of Works. It should not be impossible to assess the units of brain-work and time required for a given service, and the number of such services necessary for a given department.

A beginning in this direction has, however, been made, and in the trading accounts and balance sheets, the Army Ordnance Factories Account, the Navy Dockyard Expense Account, and the reports on the work of various other departments, it is possible to acquire a good deal of information as to comparative costs. This information is, however, not concentrated ; on the contrary, it is diffused through a number of volumes, the bulk of many

[1] *See* Second Report of Public Accounts Committee, 1925.

of which deal with non-financial questions. But though no doubt many more comparisons of cost could be made between departments, it is probably true to say that the Treasury is the only possible controller of day-to-day expenditure in detail, and that the task of vouching for the fact that the government has obtained value for its money in every particular is altogether outside the function of the Comptroller and Auditor-General.[1]

It has been stated that the work of auditing the national accounts is a continuous process. Throughout the year the auditors are busy examining expenditure as soon as it has been incurred, and all questionable items brought to light are entered on their books. Many of these queries can be settled very quickly ; others may require the attention of the Comptroller himself; comparatively few are ultimately brought to the bar of the Public Accounts Committee. A threat of an appeal to that tribunal is still the Comptroller's most powerful weapon in the task of ensuring financial regularity and economy.

The Public Accounts Committee is a committee of the House of Commons, appointed at the beginning of each session in accordance with a standing order. It consists of fifteen members. Its task is the ' examination of the accounts showing the appropriation of the sums granted by Parliament to meet public expenditure.' Its chairman is generally a distinguished representative of the opposition, often a former Financial Secretary to the Treasury, and the actual Financial Secretary to the Treasury is only a private member of it. Its

[1] *See* Sir M. Ramsay's evidence before the Select Committee on Procedure on Public Business, 1931.

service, though onerous, is sought after. Many distinguished men have sat on it. Party differences affect it little. Meeting year after year, sitting in private, withdrawn from clamour and publicity, its members acquire a sense of corporate responsibility and corporate self-respect. It was instituted by Gladstone in 1861, and is reappointed every year soon after the session begins. Its work is perhaps the most valuable part of parliamentary control of finance. True, it does not sit till long after the money has been spent. But it renders future misfeasance more difficult. Its business is to see that all parliamentary grants, including supplementary grants, have been applied to the objects which Parliament prescribed. But in reality it does more. It looks into causes as well as consequences. It censures improper expenditure as well as improper accounting. It exposes waste and inefficiency. It has before it the reports of the Comptroller and Auditor-General, and with these in view it carefully examines the accounts, administering advice, reproof, and, by disallowing a charge, even punishment should it be necessary. The Comptroller and Auditor-General sits with it: so does a high Treasury official. Disagreements are rare, either among its members or with the Comptroller or with the Treasury. Nearly all its enquiries, indeed, are on points raised by the Comptroller, one more proof of the usefulness of this high officer of the House of Commons. It can call for any papers, and it examines the Accounting Officers who, having signed the Appropriation Accounts, are responsible for their correctness. It questions them as to the expenditure of the grants in their charge, and the Accounting Officers have to justify and explain the payments made by their departments. It will be remembered that they are themselves personally responsible for all expenditure from the grant, and unless some payment has been authorised by their superior against their advice and in face of their written objection, the blame for misapplication or misspending of public money falls upon their heads. The practice of appointing a high officer, often the permanent head of the department, as Accounting Officer is of great assistance to the examination of the committee. For such a person is conversant with the policy of the department, and knows the reasons which led to the adoption of a particular course of action. He can put the case of the department with knowledge and understanding. In addition to the examination of the Accounting Officers, the committee can call any other witness and examine him personally. Such examinations can be a most unpleasant ordeal for the official concerned.

When it has finished its scrutiny, the Public Accounts Committee reports to Parliament. These reports are exceedingly frank and plain-spoken. On their receipt, there are two ways in which the sinner may be brought to book. The report can, and should, be discussed in the House of Commons. Very seldom is it discussed. Want of time, lateness in the session, the fact that the misdeeds disclosed are ancient history, and the natural wish of governments to escape blame, all tend to prevent it, and no debates on their reports have taken place since the war. But there is another method, very effective and always used, Treasury censure. The Treasury do not spare the rod. The committee's reports are driven home with force and energy. A Treasury minute, reporting what action has been taken, is presented to Parliament. The Treasury have probably been preaching the same sermon before, but their hearers have not listened. Now it is not they who thunder, but the mighty House of Commons.

The only shackle on the efficacy of the Public Accounts Committee is the late date at which they can operate. We are now in the financial year 1931. The estimates laid before the House of Commons in February 1930 have been prepared in November or December 1929. They cover a year which, beginning 1st April 1930, ends 31st March, 1931. When it has closed, the Appropriation Accounts will be got out, but so great is the work involved that they will not be presented to the House till January or February 1932 when the Public Accounts Committee will get to work on them. The committee will then be criticising expenditure which in fact was crystallised nearly two and a half years earlier. Their enquiry is perhaps an inquest. But inquests have their value. They detect crime and disclose disease.

CHAPTER VIII

PUBLIC ECONOMY

THE final report of the Public Accounts Committee closes the long-drawn-out financial process. The methods whereby the state decides on its expenditure, and those by which the money is provided to meet it, have now been studied. The checks and controls upon the executive's power to make use of public money have also been examined in all their detail. The question that next requires an answer is, How far is the complicated system effective? Does the existing financial machinery ensure that money taken from the taxpayer is spent by the government in the most productive and efficient manner? It is the executive who draw up the plan of the national expenditure, but this plan has to be submitted to the House of Commons before it can be put into operation, and the manner of its execution is subsequently criticised by the Comptroller and Auditor-General and the Public Accounts Committee. The control over the executive is theoretically strong, but how far is it real and useful in practice, and to what extent do the efforts of the Cabinet, the Treasury and the House of Commons ensure a wise and economic outlay of public money?

First of all, however, it is well to step aside for a moment to consider what constitutes wise expenditure on the part of a state. Governments spend money in order to provide services. There are two points to be considered. First, a question of policy – what services should be provided ; and this implies a balancing of the cost of the service against the benefit derived from it. And secondly, a question of management – how can the money laid out upon a service be spent to the best advantage ? Wise expenditure depends upon a competent decision, both as to the services provided and as to the way the money is spent. The first problem presents itself to the statesman in a much more complicated form than that which confronts the individual ; for the income of the latter is limited and so is his life ; he does not have to look far ahead, and there can be an immediate balancing of utility against cost. There is no such hard and fast limit to the state's income, and none to the state's life. It has to think of the advantage to the future, as well as to the present generation, and the balancing of benefit against cost is far more difficult. The cost is the burden of taxation, and it is hard to assess this, and harder still to balance it against a service, the result of which is spread over many years and divided amongst many classes. Those who bear the burden may not derive the benefit ; they certainly will not do so in the same proportion. Consequently the value of any service is not easy to determine, and to fix upon that scheme of services which can most profitably be provided by the state is an extraordinarily difficult problem. The cause of economy is served when the choice is well made. It is not necessarily furthered by refraining from expenditure ; that may prove a wasteful and short-sighted course. A wise answer to the question what services should be given is therefore the essential foundation to the proper management of national finance. Less important, but still necessary if the public finances are to be properly administered, is a successful answer to the second question. How can the money provided for a service be spent to the best advantage? The measure of efficient expenditure which competition offers in business is not available to the state. Consequently both aspects of state expenditure, the manner as well as the object, present problems which have to be solved without the help of comparison or analogy.

With these two questions constantly in mind, it is possible to examine the methods of the various authorities who control or criticise the financial proposals of the government, and to endeavour to arrive at some idea of the value of their services to the cause of economy. By far the most important of these authorities is the House of Commons. In considering the control exercised by that body over finance, a distinction must be drawn between control over taxation and control over expenditure. The old quarrel between Parliament and Crown was over the right to tax. This quarrel was settled by the Civil War, and the sole right of the Commons to levy taxation was confirmed after the Revolution of 1688 and has never been questioned since. But, in the early days of the struggle, the Commons claimed no supervision over expenditure. The King must remedy grievances before he obtained supply: but the object of the Commons was to buy that remedy as cheaply as possible, and, once the money was paid over, it did not concern itself with the use to which it was put. If the King spent it on a foreign war, such is the habit of kings: if he wasted it on less reputable activities, might he not do as he willed with his own?[1] As constitutional government was slowly evolved, as more and more of the executive powers of the Crown passed to its ministers, as those ministers gradually became entirely responsible to Parliament, speaking in the King's name, it is true, but by one of our delightful fictions representing in reality the views of the House of Commons or of the constituencies which might be quite different, the distinction still remained. Governments maintained a tighter hold over expenditure than over taxation. On taxation the House of Commons, apart from the government, always had a weighty voice. And it has to the present day. It is a well-known constitutional practice, for example, that a government can afford to be beaten on the details of a tax and not resign. It can always find the money in some other way. But rarely can a government suffer defeat on expenditure, and then on very minor matters only. If beaten, it resigns. And, if we look beyond Parliament to the electorate, we cannot fail to see that much more interest is taken in taxation than in expenditure. Everyone tries to reduce the burden which he finds onerous, be it sur-tax or the duty on tobacco. The electorate has a greater say over taxation than over expenditure. And so has the House of Commons. It is as though ministers said to it, as kings said to earlier Parliaments: If you give me the money, please yourselves how you find it.

Even over taxation, the supervision of the House of Commons is lessening, for less and less is the House a body which stands apart from the government and criticises it. During the eighteenth

[1] Nevertheless, the first Appropriation Bill arose from the fact that moneys voted for the Dutch war were applied to far less reputable purposes!

century, and up to the Reform Act of 1832, it was a chamber which contained members who, though nominally either Tory or Whig, were ready to pay more attention to individual argument than to claims of party. Since the passage of the first Reform Bill, party has exercised an ever increasing influence over the individual member. Moreover, there is another factor. Wise criticism of taxation must spring from a balancing of the burden against the value of the service rendered, and to do this the critic must know the weight of the burden. But Parliament has become less representative of the citizen as a taxpayer than it used to be. No doubt in the unreformed Parliament neither industry nor wealth, unless it were landed wealth, received their fair representation : but the very fact that many boroughs were rotten and privately owned made them purchasable, and did, by a devious and unsavoury path, result in taxable wealth being represented. Now, however, owing to subsequent extensions of the franchise, a change is apparent. Large bodies of the electorate consider, on the one hand, that other classes do or ought to bear the bulk of the burden, and on the other are calling out for increased expenditure. This demand reacts on members, and on members of all parties, not of one alone, with the consequence that the House of Commons becomes less and less the watchdog of the taxpayer.

But still, after discounting this, the House of Commons, representing the electorate, can make its wishes very forcibly known to governments, and compel them to listen to it upon taxation. It carries a very real weight. Moreover, tax questions excite interest, and are debated with information and fairness. Altogether, in spite of the overwhelming power of governments, the House of Commons, either directly or indirectly, does supply upon taxation that external critical authority which all governments need.

But it cannot be repeated too often that taxation is conditioned by expenditure, and therefore the power of the House of Commons in the matter of taxes does not take it very far. What is its position with regard to expenditure? Here the distinction which we noted between the two aspects of expenditure must be kept in mind. The House of Commons is a body highly competent to judge the objects of expenditure, but it is ill-suited to criticise its manner. The first is a question of policy. The government draws up a scheme of the services which it proposes to provide out of public money, and the House can judge this scheme on its merits. It can weigh the value of the services against the cost. Moreover, it can express its judgment without the certainty of provoking resignation. For on such questions, though matters of high policy, governments are more ready to accept the decision of a hostile House. A measure can scarcely be rejected, but it can be altered out of recognition, and the government need not resign. Consequently, on the question of what services should be provided, the opinion of the House of Commons carries real weight. Its influence may be used more often in favour of spending than of saving, but still the private member is in the position to form and to express a judgment. If a government propose to give pensions to widows, the advantage can be placed on one side and the cost on the other. The question is put in a simple form: Is the benefit worth the cost ? with the further question, Can the country afford it ? On such questions the House is as competent to decide as any body in the world. It is more difficult for it, however, to give a judgment on the extension or curtailment of an existing service. The fact of its existence is strong evidence that it is necessary, and the only question is whether it is too big or too small. This is a hard matter to judge. The private member cannot easily determine the proper size of an essential service, such as the army, and on such an issue the government cannot afford to be beaten. If beaten, it must resign. In such discussions it is hard for the House either to stand apart from the government, or to possess materials for effective criticism. The government knows so much more.

But it is on the second question – How can the money be laid out to the best advantage ? – that the House of Commons is really ineffective. The estimates are made up by the departments and the Treasury. They show the cost of running each service in detail, though, as we have seen, the form in which they are presented does not facilitate criticism. And it is here that criticism is needed. We want to know that no more is spent on a service than is required, that daily administration is economical, that the staff of an office is equated to the work to be done. But it is at this point that parliamentary control breaks down. The House of Commons cannot provide the criticism which is needed. All the influences mentioned above, which incline members to give a favourable eye to expenditure, unfit them to be stern judges of the daily cost of running the government. Indeed, it is hardly too much to say that the House is unsuited to pass such judgments because it wants expenditure. For one suggestion for saving you have ten for spending. This is no vice of the House of Commons. It is the temper of the times. And therefore at the outset the House generally is unfitted to be a critic. But the matter does not rest there. Had it the best will in the world it has little power. For one thing, the estimates do not offer the private member material on which to form an opinion. For another, he has not sufficient knowledge. He only knows what he can pick up from outside. The minister has a skilled staff behind him and all the requisite information at his service : that makes the attack difficult, but what renders it nearly hopeless is that the defendant has been through it all before. It is perfectly certain that the attacker can raise no point which the minister has not himself examined with his officials, or which the Treasury have not queried. The material has been sifted through a finer sieve than any which the House of Commons can apply. The private member is further handicapped in that he comes too late. The government have fixed upon the estimates many months before the discussion, and in their decision the House of Commons took no part. It was then that economy was made or marred, for having once published the estimates to the world the government stand or fall by them. Governments are too strong. They use their strength to the full. If a vote on a big estimate is rejected or reduced, they resign. This looks like accepting the will of the House, but in reality is bludgeoning it. If the Government wanted to bow its head it should consent to the rejection of the expenditure. By threatening to resign, it puts to its supporters the alternative of either swallowing an expenditure they dislike, or of turning them out, with the consequence that a hostile government is put in power, or a general election is entailed, with all its expense, toil and uncertainty, or else both evils fall together on the unlucky private member. Faced with this choice of evils, he chooses what he thinks the lesser. He votes for the expenditure. He does not wish to turn out a government in other respects so admirable. He is not allowed to stand critically apart and pass judgment on finance alone. The government throw a sword into the scale. You need never listen to a critic unless he can be unpleasant if you do not, and they make it nearly impossible for the House of Commons to be such a critic, except in rare and extraordinary circumstances. The result is that once expenditure appears in an estimate it nearly always passes.

It may be thought that this is a debased and cynical view to take of the House of Commons. It may be said that members should regard themselves as representing all interests : that they should consider the taxpayer, and above all should never forget the reaction of high taxation on industry, on prices, and in fact on all branches of national life : and that they should not carry party allegiance too far. But in truth the view is neither sordid nor untrue. No one can have been a member of Parliament without coming away with an immense respect for that body. No legislature in the world is its equal in impartiality or in critical ability. But to try to erect it into a critic of the daily expenditure of a government is to ask it to do work for which by constitution and by circumstance it is unfitted. It chooses a government. If that government were wildly extravagant, it could and would turn it out. For the most part it prefers to trust it.

Indeed, the shortcomings of the House of Commons have been pointed out in words far more forcible than those used above. Sir Herbert Samuel, who has had long experience as a member of parliament, as a minister and as Chairman of the Select Committee on National Expenditure, wrote as follows: 'So far as the direct control of expenditure is concerned, the estimates might as well not be submitted to Parliament at all.'[1] Sir E. Hilton Young, one of the ablest of Financial Secretaries to the Treasury, says that 'Once the estimates have been published the taxpayer's fate is sealed.'[2] That the House of Commons does not supervise expenditure in detail is shown by the fact that half the yearly estimates are passed undiscussed. That it could not do so is equally apparent. Opinion on this point is weighty and unanimous.

Attempts have been made to give the House of Commons more material for criticism and more power to enforce it. For instance, before a government move a Financial Resolution (*see* p. 37) they are pledged to circulate a White Paper, giving an explanation and the amount of the proposed charge. This is valuable, for the amount of money involved is not usually stated in the resolution, and for this reason, and also because parliamentary terminology does not make criticism easy, examination of it was difficult formerly. This concession, which was recommended in the Ninth Report of the Select Committee on National Expenditure, is perhaps a slight one, but it is in the right direction.

[1] *See* his Introduction to *Parliament and the Taxpayer*, by E. H. Davenport, 1918.

[2] *System of National Finance*, p. 23.

So also is the rule enforced since 1926 that every bill must be prefaced by a note as to the estimated cost to the state (including that of probable additions to staff) of the proposals it contains. So much for material. As to power, three reforms attempt this. One has failed. The others have succeeded, and succeeded to a degree which is perhaps not realised. The first, the failure, is the setting up of the Estimates Committee: the successes are the appointment of the Comptroller and Auditor-General, and the Public Accounts Committee.

The Estimates Committee is a committee of fifteen members of the House, drawn from all parties. They were first appointed in the session 1912–13. They can examine any estimate they like and report what economies may be effected therein 'consistent with the policy implied in these estimates.' These are limiting words: the committee cannot discuss policy: it cannot say, for example, that we are building too many cruisers: all it can ensure is that not too much money has been allotted, and that it is being prudently spent. Now all big expenditure comes from policy, and this the committee cannot discuss. Moreover, it is advisory only: it cannot, like the French Budget Committee, reject an estimate and bring in a new one. Its criticism does not condemn the minister in charge, nor does its approval absolve him of responsibility. But above all, it appears too late on the scene. It does not examine the estimate till long after it has been presented. For the reasons given above, it cannot then be altered. Consequently the Estimates Committee has proved of little use as an instrument of economy.

But fortunately this is not the case with the Comptroller and Auditor-General nor with the

Public Accounts Committee. Working hand in hand they have undoubtedly added to the control which the House of Commons can exercise over finance. They are not concerned with the formulation of policy nor with the type of economy which springs therefrom. But in this matter the House itself, as we have seen, is in a position to exercise a powerful influence over governments. But the Public Accounts Committee with the help of the Comptroller and Auditor-General is able to provide a criticism on the outlay of public money, and this is the aspect of expenditure where criticism is more particularly needed. It is true that they are primarily concerned to see that government expenditure is confined to the schedule approved by Parliament, but this part of their work, though of fundamental importance in our financial system, is by no means their only function. The safeguards against misapplication of public money are so complete that it is now almost impossible for a government to spend without the authority of Parliament. The danger is that with the authority of Parliament they may spend in an uneconomic way, and it is in criticisms of the lack of economy that the work of the Comptroller and Auditor-General and of the Public Accounts Committee is particularly valuable.

The work of the Comptroller and the Public Accounts Committee has already been fully described, and their growing tendency to criticise the nature of expenditure noted. Though discussing expenditure already incurred, the committee exercises considerable influence, not, it is true, over the current year's expenditure, which is already settled before the committee starts on its work, but over that for future years, and above all it acts as a valuable medium for publicity. The mere fact that public attention is called to what the committee considers uneconomic expenditure often effects a cure.

Such are the powers of the House of Commons with regard to finance. On questions of policy it is in a position to pass judgment and to make its decisions effective. But, even taking into account the Comptroller and the Public Accounts Committee, it must be admitted that the House of Commons has very little control over the way – inefficient or economic – in which public money is spent. It cannot be certain that contracts are not too high, labour costs excessive, offices overstaffed. For the efficient solution of such problems, and for all economies in day-to-day administration, the House of Commons must rely on the Treasury, and the departments themselves. Within the departments economy mainly depends on the parliamentary chief, the Accounting Officer and the permanent head, if these last two appointments are not combined in one individual. Perhaps the parliamentary chief has least influence over economy. It might be thought that he bears the same relation to his Permanent Secretary as the board of directors of a big enterprise bear to their business manager, and that, if the one system results in efficiency and economy, the other should also. But this analogy, as do all analogies between government and private enterprise, breaks down at the start, for a board of directors have two powers which do not belong to a minister. They can judge their manager's work by the definite measure of money profit : government offices produce no profit. They can dismiss their manager : a civil servant's rights are, quite properly, protected more strongly. Therefore, though the influence of an able, broad-minded and experienced man of affairs at the head of a government office may be immense, though he may exercise a great power for good over the whole of the staff under him, he has neither the measure nor the control which an ordinary employer possesses. Consequently economy must be left almost entirely to the Permanent Secretary, who is also probably the Accounting Officer. A Permanent Secretary is moved by two influences: an honest belief in the importance of his office and the desirability of extending its beneficent activities, and an honest desire to economise. Without the first he is uninspired, without the second he may be expensive. His action is the result of the two conflicting attractions. If the permanent head of a department is competent and so inclined, he has considerable scope for making the expenditure of his department efficient. But there is no acid-test of competition by which he can be judged to anything like the same extent as can the manager of a commercial concern, though the Treasury have a very good idea of the relative efficiency of the various heads of departments. It is greatly to the credit of the public service that, tested by any standard, very few of these officers would fail.

But while each department is naturally impressed with the value of its own activities, the Treasury must co-ordinate the expenditure of all. It must see that lavish cost in one direction does not involve starvation in another. It has to consider the work of all departments and is able to form a shrewd idea of the money required for the service rendered. It scrutinises every item in the estimates submitted by the departments and its sanction must be obtained before any new charge can be included. This gives it a very real control over expenditure, and it is in a position to bring expert knowledge to the examination. Seeing the estimates of all spending departments year after year, the Controller of Supply Services and his experts, the Treasury officers of accounts, can compare costs in different years and in different departments. The Controller is thus able to form a fairly accurate judgment as to what costs are excessive and what are justifiable. The Controller of Establishments can at once put his finger on a case of redundant staff. He is the final arbiter of the establishments of all the departments. Thus through its highly trained personnel, its long experience, and its power to take a general survey, the Treasury carries a weight even greater than its wide actual powers. Its control rests not on rules only, but on character and influence, and the continual insistence on economical management and frugal spending. But the Treasury cannot be stronger than its Chancellor, and here we come back to the government again. For the Chancellor is a member of the government, and without his support Treasury control cannot be made effective. If he allows the First Lord of the Admiralty or the Minister of Health, or whoever at that moment may be the most clamorous raider on the public purse, to over-persuade or overbear him in enforcing economy, the work of the Treasury falls to nothing and the watchman has wakened in vain. And the Prime Minister must support the Chancellor. He, of course, must view all subjects from a wide standpoint. Economy, with its consequences in the reduction of taxation, is but one of many factors. He cannot always yield to the

Chancellor's pleading. But what he can and should do is to help as far as he can.

Great is the power of governments, and any one of them that wants to economise has, in the civil service and the Treasury, a most efficient instrument at command. Under a prudent administration, efficiency and cheapness are well combined. But if the policy of a government is not economical the House of Commons will not change it. Since the war there has been much talk of saving, and the costs of administration have been very satisfactorily reduced. That has been the work of the civil service and Treasury, moved and aided by a large body of opinion both inside and outside the House of Commons. Yet the fact remains that the national expenditure, after falling for some years, has again leapt upwards with startling rapidity. The blame for this, if blame there be, must rest on the House of Commons that approved a whole series of new and costly services. Once these policies are approved, the work of the Treasury and the departments is confined to seeing that that policy is economically carried out, and in that task they have certainly not failed.

Such is our machinery for economy. No one, either student or politician, regards it as perfect. Reform is difficult: for no government, of whatever colour, consents to divide its sovereignty, and unless it does, it confers nothing of value on the House of Commons or any committee of it. The problem is narrow: if governments want more than advice, if they desire a critic who can enforce his objection, they alone can create him. It is no use clamouring for the critic and at the same time making certain that he is still-born.

PART II

CURRENCY

CHAPTER IX

GREAT BRITAIN'S CURRENCY SYSTEM

BEFORE the war a chapter dealing with the currency system would have been considered out of place in a book of this character. At that time the amount of currency in circulation at any given time was not controlled by the government, but was automatically dependent on the amount of gold in the country. A partial return to pre-war conditions was made in 1926, but during the last few months the government has again been compelled to take a hand in attempting to solve acute and vital problems which arose, at any rate in part, from a currency crisis. Under these circumstances some account of the history of Great Britain's modern currency system is essential to the proper survey of the government's finances.

The Bank Act of 1844 may be taken as the starting-point of the modern currency system. Before that time any bank might issue its own notes, and banknotes being only promises to pay legal tender at sight (legal tender at that time being gold), banks frequently failed to meet their obligations and the public suffered. The act of 1844 regulated the note issue in the first place by confining the right to issue notes to existing banks, and, secondly, by encouraging all banks to merge their issues in that of the Bank of England, thereby practically conferring a monopoly on that institution. The act further proceeded to lay down the conditions on which the Bank of England should proceed. A note-issuing department was to be set up, distinct from the banking branch. Securities to the amount of fourteen million pounds were to be transferred from the banking department to the issue department, together with so much of the gold coin and gold and silver bullion as were not required for banking purposes. In return, the banking department was to receive notes to such an amount as, when added to the notes in circulation, would make the total note issue of the bank equal to the amount of the securities, coin and bullion transferred to the issue department.

Furthermore, any notes issued in the future were to be covered pound for pound by gold, with the exception that two-thirds of any country banknote issue lapsing might be re-issued by the Bank of England against securities, and, further, that one-fifth of the bullion held as cover for notes might be silver bullion. Finally, the bank was put under a statutory obligation to buy bullion at a specified price.

Few acts of Parliament which have roused such deep differences of opinion during their passage have proved more useful in operation. It is true that between 1844 and 1866 the act had to be suspended three times, but, once the system had settled down, it worked without further hitch until the outbreak of war in 1914.

Whether the act would have worked quite so smoothly if great economies had not been made in the use of gold, as by the invention of the cheque, is now a point of purely academic interest. The fact remains that in 1914 the country had enjoyed nearly fifty years without a currency crisis ; that the bank, by a manipulation of the rate charged to would-be borrowers, could control the influx and efflux of gold to such good purpose that the nation could afford, what now would be an undreamt-of extravagance, the luxury of a gold coinage. The majority of ready money transactions were actually settled in gold, and everyone who possessed a Bank of England note (issued in no denomination lower than five pounds) could at sight change that note to gold. Since 1861 the Bank of England had ceased to use its right to base a proportion of its note issue on silver, and, except for £18,450,000 issued against securities, the whole note issue was covered by gold.

Not that this implied an enormous accumulation of gold in the country ; rather the reverse. It has been estimated that on 30th June, 1914, the Bank of England had issued in round numbers thirty-eight million pounds' worth of notes which had a gold covering, and that there were some one hundred and twenty-three million pounds' worth of gold coin either in the vaults of the various joint stock banks or in circulation. The pre-war strength of the City of London lay in England's being a very large creditor nation, and acting as the world's banker. A rise in the bank rate, if pushed far enough, could be relied upon to draw gold to London. During the American crisis of 1907 a heavy strain was put on London's reserves, which was met by drawing gold from sixteen or seventeen different countries. At that time London was a completely free gold centre, where notes could be exchanged at any time for bullion, and that bullion, if taken to the Mint, could be changed into sovereigns without charge.

Then came the war. The Bank Act was suspended, though in fact the suspension was of practical use only for a very few days, since the Treasury decided to become responsible for the nation's currency. The bank continued to issue its notes on its statutory basis, but the Treasury also issued currency notes of the value of one pound and ten shillings, replacing the golden sovereigns and half-sovereigns, which people were urged to pay into their banks, whence they passed into the hands of the Treasury, to be used for war payments abroad. As until March 1919 Great Britain, thanks largely to the physical impossibility of exporting gold, was able to remain nominally on the gold standard, these Treasury notes were technically convertible into gold, but the very rapid expansion of credit, and the consequent growth in the amount of currency required, soon in reality divorced the note from gold. Treasury issues of notes took place under the Currency and Bank Notes Act, 1914, and the actual machinery of the issue is worthy of study. It would, of course, have been perfectly simple for the Treasury to print notes and pay their bills with them, but notes issued under those conditions would scarcely have inspired much confidence, and confidence was essential to the success of the undertaking. The ordinary Englishman was accustomed to accepting a Bank of England note as the equivalent of gold, and it was imperative that he should as readily accept the Treasury note, which was originally intended to cover the awkward period likely to arise immediately after the outbreak of war, when it was supposed that nervous citizens might be inclined to realise their assets and withdraw their deposits from the banks. These latter institutions, therefore, might have required a larger supply of cash than they usually carried, and the Bank of England would have been unable to satisfy their demands without a suspension of the Bank Act. At the same time, to prevent an undue amount of bullion being minted and put into circulation, a note of smaller denomination than the five-pound note was required, and, as has been stated, it was this smaller note that the Treasury decided to issue, the suspension of the Bank Act being only actually effective before and until supplies of the new notes were available.

The notes originally were issued through the Bank of England to the joint stock banks to a limit not exceeding, in the maximum, 20 per cent. of the liabilities of each bank on current and deposit accounts. The amount of the notes so issued to each bank was to be treated as an advance, which was to bear interest at current bank rate. In the event when, after a four day moratorium, the banks reopened, there was very little panic, the crisis passed, and the banks paid off the notes that had been advanced by the Treasury. They paid off these advances by transferring the requisite portion of their balances at the Bank of England to the credit of the Treasury, for, of course, a certain number of the new notes had been put into circulation. These credits went into a new account opened by the Treasury at the Bank of England, called the Currency Notes Redemption Account, which, therefore, possessed as an asset a credit at the Bank of England equivalent to its total liability, namely, the amount of notes issued. So far the issue of the new notes had not apparently changed the currency position of the nation. All that had happened was that when the joint stock banks, to meet the demands of their customers for cash, wished to replenish their tills, they had drawn Treasury notes through the Bank of England instead of gold or notes from the Bank, and had transferred some of the cash reserves which they kept at the Bank to the government. But from the point of view of the Bank there was a change, for, when the joint stock banks required cash, instead of losing gold or notes – that is to say, part of its reserve – the Bank of England merely transferred a credit in its books from the joint stock bank concerned to the Currency Notes Redemption Account. A check on credit inflation was thereby removed, for the measure of inflation was the gold reserve of the Bank. At the same time, no inflation need necessarily have followed the issue of notes of smaller denomination than that of five pounds. If the government had left the credit balance of the Currency Notes Redemption Account lying idle at the Bank, no increase in the amount of cash in circulation, nor assets on which fresh credits could be based, would have occurred ; but a government does not leave any of its funds idle. A small credit working balance had, of course, to be maintained, because notes were returned, and when returned had to be paid off. The process of repayment was exactly the reverse of that of issue. If the joint stock banks had more notes than they required for their day-to-day reserves of legal tender, they paid them back into the Bank of England. The Bank, however, kept no currency notes in its reserves. The returned notes, therefore, were cancelled, and the returning bank was credited with their value, the Currency Notes Redemption Account being debited with the like amount. Apart from the balance used in this manner, the bulk of the credits obtained from the sale of currency notes were invested in government securities, which thus formed the principal assets of the fund. A great part of these were, of course, in a very liquid and easily realisable form, for only thus could the account be worked with a small credit balance. The interest earned on investments and advances formed a part of the assets of the Currency Notes Redemption Account. As it accrued it was paid into a special fund, known as the Investments Reserve Account. A part of this fund was kept as a reserve against the depreciation of securities held against currency notes, and the remainder (with the exception of a small balance) was paid into the Consolidated Fund.

This process of investment and profit-earning at first sight looks good business for the state, but, unfortunately, it is only the beginning of a vicious circle. For the funds obtained by the government in return for the sale of securities to the Currency Notes Redemption Account were transferred to the Consolidated Fund, and immediately drawn upon to pay for some of the many expenses of the government. The paymaster's drafts were paid into the bank balances of their various recipients, and ended in increasing the total balances which the banks concerned kept at the Bank of England. Such balances are regarded by those banks as cash, and the foundation for fresh credit. Thus by borrowing the money paid to them as the purchase price of currency notes, and by spending the money so borrowed, the government swelled the accounts of the joint stock banks at the Bank of England, with the result that the banks were able to create fresh credit on their increased cash reserves, on the basis of, roughly, eight pounds of credit for one of cash. The amount of money in circulation was thereby increased, for a grant of credit stimulated the demand for more legal tender. The banks bought more Treasury notes, the government exchanged the credits so obtained by the Currency Notes Redemption Account for securities, spent the credits so obtained, and so the whole process went on over and over again. In 1918 a committee, appointed, under the chairmanship of the late Lord Cunliffe, 'to consider the various problems which will arise in connection with currency and the foreign exchanges during the period of reconstruction, and report upon the steps required to bring about the restoration of normal conditions in due course,' reported. They found that on 10th July, 1918, the amount of currency notes issued but not covered by gold was £230,412,000, whereas £28,500,000 had a gold cover.

In their report the committee were strongly in favour of a speedy return to the gold standard, and as a step in this direction they recommended that, after the war, there should be a legal limitation of the note issue. At the close of 1919 the Treasury acted on this recommendation, and ruled (Treasury Minute, 15th December, 1919) that 'the actual maximum fiduciary circulation of currency notes in any year shall be the fixed maximum for the following year.' As a result of this ruling the amount of currency notes which could be issued without a gold backing was no longer unlimited. The limit became the maximum number of uncovered notes that were issued in the previous year. The depression set in soon after this ruling was given, and during its course the limit was not effective. For the contraction of credit resulted in a decreased demand for currency, and the banks, in fact, asked for fewer notes than they could have obtained under the legal limitation. With reviving trade, however, the limitation began to be of practical importance. The Bank of England was bound to supply legal tender to the banks when they decided to draw on their balances in that form. The Treasury might not supply more than the fixed number of currency notes unbacked by gold or by Bank of England notes. Consequently if the joint stock banks were to apply for a number of notes greater than the maximum fiduciary issue, the Bank would supply them, but the Treasury would hold Bank of England notes against the additional currency notes issued. That is to say, instead of buying securities with the credit placed to the account of the Currency Notes Redemption Fund by the issue of these notes, it would take banknotes or gold from the Bank of England. This would affect the Bank's reserve in the same way that the withdrawal of gold would have done under the pre-war system, and if the process continued, and the reserves were seriously diminished, the Bank would have to take steps to reduce the amount of credit outstanding. Thus when the amount of currency notes in circulation approached the legal maximum, the issue became a matter which affected the position of the Bank of England, and in order to protect its reserve the Bank had to step in and take control of the situation.[1]

Between 1919 and 1925 great efforts were made to reduce the amount of the fiduciary issue,[2] and these efforts, assisted by the trade slump of 1921–4, were attended by a considerable measure of success. On 31st December, 1925, the enactment whereby the free export of gold was prohibited was due to expire. The government of the day decided not to renew it. On 28th April, 1925, Mr. Churchill, in the course of his budget speech, announced that, although legally not bound to return to a free gold market until the end of the year, the government would by a general licence enable the Bank of England to export gold from the following day. The passage of the Gold Standard Act followed, receiving the royal assent on 13th May, 1925. Under the terms of that act the Bank of England was, so long as Sub-section (1) of Section 1 of the act (the contents of which will be described presently) remained in force, to sell to anyone who might choose to demand it, bullion at the rate of £3 17*s* 10½*d*. per ounce troy of gold of standard fineness. Provided, however, that no demand need legally be met if it were for less than four

[1] The amount of currency notes in circulation between the years 1920 and 1927 was as follows (in round figures):

1920	310 million pounds	1924	263 million pounds
1921	311 " "	1925	267 " "
1922	279 " "	1926	278 " "
1923	265 " "	1927	275 " "

The legal maximum of uncovered notes for the three last years was:

1925	248 million pounds.	1926	247 million pounds
1927	246 million pounds		

In December 1926 the fiduciary note issue came within £45,000 of its maximum legal limit.

[2] In 1920 the amount of notes issued (including Bank of England notes) was 449 million pounds, of which 138 millions were covered by gold, leaving a fiduciary issue of 310 millions. In 1925 the total amount of notes issued was 399 millions, of which 152 millions were covered, leaving a fiduciary issue of 245 millions.

hundred ounces troy, or a multiple of that amount. London, therefore, could scarcely be said to be returning to its position as a free market for gold, but the act of 1925 was, as far as the export of gold was concerned, a step in that direction. Moreover, to consolidate the gold of the country in the hands of the Bank, the government paid over 27 million pounds' worth of metal held in the Currency Notes Redemption Account, receiving banknotes in return. Further to safeguard the exchange value of the pound sterling, the Treasury was, by Section 2 of the act, enabled to borrow for exchange purposes. It is, however, Sub-section (1) of Section 1 that demonstrates how very partial was the return to the gold standard as it was understood before the war. By that sub-section, until a proclamation to the contrary effect should be issued, the Bank of England should be under no obligation to pay gold coin for its notes. Moreover, the right which had theoretically existed since 1914 of their holders converting currency notes into gold coins at will was revoked, and no gold was in future to be coined at the Mint unless the bullion was taken there by the Bank of England. These drastic precautions, more drastic in theory than in practice, were deemed necessary to protect from frivolous dispersal in small hoards the Bank's store of gold, which, including the state's contribution of 27 million pounds, amounted to about 180 millions. After ten years the majority of the people were not likely suddenly to change their habits and revert to the use of gold coin, but there would no doubt have been many who would have returned to their former customs, and it was thought wise to prevent the dissipation of the Bank's reserve, the main function of which was to protect the exchange value of the pound sterling.

It will be noted that the Gold Standard Act, 1925, did not make any provision for the transfer of the currency note issue to the Bank of England. The reason for this was that the government had decided, in conformity with the recommendations of the Cunliffe Committee, that it was desirable to have practical experience of the working of the gold standard under the new conditions before making the Bank of England responsible for the issue of currency notes. In fact, three years elapsed before the note issue was so transferred. The Currency and Bank Notes Act, 1928, received the royal assent on 2nd July of that year. Under its provisions, on a day to be fixed by Order in Council, all currency notes certified by the Treasury to be outstanding on that day were for all legal purposes to be deemed to be banknotes, and the Bank of England was to become liable for them, and power to issue notes for one pound and ten shillings was accordingly conferred on the Bank, such notes to be legal tender for the payment of any amount, including the payment of banknotes by the Bank. Banknotes might be issued to an amount representing the gold coin and gold bullion for the time being in the issue department, and, in addition 260 million pounds' worth in excess of the gold cover, the latter, of course, being the fiduciary issue for which silver to the value of five and a half million pounds might be held, the remainder being covered by securities.[1] On the day appointed for the transfer of the currency note issue to the Bank,

[1] Critics, perhaps wise after the event, have asserted that the fiduciary issue was too large. At one period, while the Bank lost 60 millions in gold, the amount of currency in circulation increased by 32 millions. London thus, it is argued, lost its ability to deflate and sell goods.

all the assets of the Currency Notes Redemption Account, other than government securities, were to be transferred to the issue department of the Bank, and if, after this had been done, the amount of notes outstanding exceeded the assets so transferred, government securities to the requisite amount necessary to balance the account were also to be transferred. The Treasury got a nice little windfall as a result of the Currency Notes Redemption Account being wound up, for not only were all surplus securities in the account sold and the money paid to the Exchequer, but the profits of the note issue were also to go into the Exchequer. In the year ended 31st March, 1931, the sum so paid was over six million pounds. Power was also taken under the act to arrange for either the decrease or increase of the fiduciary issue. The decrease could be arranged between the Bank and the Treasury, but if the Bank applied for an increase and got it, the necessary Treasury minute was to be laid forthwith before Parliament, and, in any case, no such authority was to be valid for more than two years from the original date of sanction unless Parliament specifically determined otherwise. The appointed day on which the act was to come into force was eventually fixed by Order in Council for 22nd November, 1928.

Such were the main terms of the act which it was hoped would rank with that of 1844. It has certainly followed precedent by having to be suspended within a comparatively short time of its passage into law. The severe slump which set in in 1929–30, and the monetary crisis in Central Europe in the spring and summer of 1931, coupled with the revelations of Great Britain's prospective budgetary deficit made by the May Committee, caused a run on London, and on the 18th September the government empowered the Bank to disregard the provisions of Sub-section 2 of Section 1 of the Gold Standard Act, 1925. This sub-section provided, as has already been explained, that the Bank should be compelled, on demand, to sell bullion in bars of four hundred ounces troy at a fixed price. The government's decision did not become generally known until the morning of Monday, 21st September. On that day Parliament was asked to pass through both Houses the Gold Standard (Amendment) Bill. Introduced into the House of Commons in the late afternoon, by eleven o'clock the same evening the bill had received the royal assent and become an Act. The main provision was that suspending the operation of Sub-section 2 of Section 1 of the Gold Standard Act, 1925, but the act also indemnified the Bank of England for any illegal action it might have taken since 18th September, and empowered the Treasury to make any regulations necessary to protect the exchange. So at the time of writing the pound sterling has been divorced from gold and again reverted to its position immediately after the war, except that the state is no longer directly responsible for any portion of the note issue. That all governments are deeply concerned in any question affecting their national currencies must be perfectly obvious : that the government has, in effect, once more taken charge of all currency problems, though perhaps not so obvious, is true. Between 1919 and 1925 all British governments strove hard to 'make the pound look the dollar in the face.' They succeeded, at the expense of British industry according to some economists, but they did succeed. All the efforts made during this period have been made in vain. What the future policy is likely to be has not yet been disclosed, but the future of the pound lies once more in the hands of the Treasury rather than in those of the Bank.

The Treasury can work towards making its value again equal to that of gold, or towards keeping it stable in terms of commodities. Anyhow, the power is theirs, and a power which could be used to maintain stable prices is one not to be discarded lightly. It is an instrument which has been put into the hands of the state by the abandonment of the gold standard. If another return is made to that standard, whether in a pre-war or a post-war sense, and the value of our currency again made dependent on the value of gold, the state will have lost a power which it might have used with great advantage to the stability of trade and the well-being of the country. Whatever the advantages of the gold standard may be, this is a factor which must be taken into account.

PART III

DEBT

CHAPTER X

NATIONAL DEBT IN GENERAL

A NATIONAL debt seems to be the price of civilisation, and yet most of the amount is represented by the cost of wars. Very little is due to remunerative purchases or beneficial undertakings. Great Britain borrowed 20 million pounds in 1836, in order to abolish slavery. The Irish famine in 1848 increased the debt by 9 millions. Disraeli paid borrowed money for the Suez Canal shares which he bought. More recently, borrowing to pay for Unemployment Insurance has added over 100 millions to the national debt. But wars represent by far the greater proportion. The Seven Years' War and various wars with France and Spain between 1688 and 1775 added 128 millions, the American War of Independence about 132 millions, and the wars with Napoleon about 607 millions. In 1816 our dead-weight debt was 846 millions ; from then down to 1914, in spite of the Crimean War, the Indian Mutiny and the South African War, it had on the whole been reduced, and on the outbreak of the Great War it stood at 651 millions. In 1920 it was 7,829 millions. Therefore the Great War added 7,178 millions to the nation's burdens.[1] Against the immense cost of war, debt spent remuneratively is a grain of sand.

[1] The figures are given in *British Finance*, 1914 to 1921, by A. W. Kirkaldy, 1921.

INTERNAL DEBT

There are different kinds of debt. The first great division is between internal and external debt, between money borrowed from British citizens, interest on which is paid in the country, and money borrowed from foreigners, whose interest is paid abroad. Since the war, for the first time in her history, Great Britain has a big external debt,[1] and this is a point the importance of which is not always recognised. What is the real difference between external and internal debt? The answer usually given is that in one case interest has to be sent abroad, while in the other case it is kept at home. Or it is said that internal debt involves a transfer only, for what is taken from people in taxes is returned to them in interest. Or it is said, picturesquely but inaccurately, that money is merely moved from one pocket to another. These statements all contain some truth. But it is necessary to probe deeper.

Assume that the Great War will mean a net loss to Great Britain of 6,000 million pounds. Assume that it will have cost that, after giving credit for what will be regained from German ships and German property and German reparations, and deducting what the Allies will repay, and the extra savings which were created through increased efforts and diminished consumption during the war. The figure is optimistic, but it will do. Of these 6,000 millions, five were borrowed at home and one in America. That also is a rough figure, but it will serve. All are lost, lost as absolutely as if the money had been blown off as fireworks. Now the

[1] On 31st March, 1931, this amounted to over 1,000 millions.

5,000 millions, which were raised here were all taken from wealth and goods and labour here. The nation is poorer by the net amount. Great Britain's productive wealth is less by that sum. And it always will be less. True, people may save, until they have built up another fund of that value, but that is making new wealth, not remaking the old. The old cannot be remade : it is destroyed, as completely as fire destroys a haystack. It has disappeared from the world, and nothing that can ever be done can recreate it.

But, that being so, the loss of the 5,000 millions of wealth is the whole loss. The fact that the 5,000 millions in question has been erected into a debt, on which interest is being paid and sinking fund is being provided, and people are being heavily taxed for these purposes, does not constitute the loss. For the money that is raised for the service of the debt is not lost to the country as the original war expenditure is lost. It is taken from one person and given to another ; and though the process of transfer may be injurious, as will be shown presently, the fact of the transfer does not diminish the total wealth of the community. That sounds paradoxical. The man who sees half his income taken away in income tax and sur-tax will exclaim that it is untrue. Without taxation there would be no loss at all, he will say. But this is not really so. It may be true in the individual case, it is not true of the country as a whole. The loss to the country is the original destruction of wealth, with the diminished productive power and depleted capital reserves which that entails. The fact that that lost wealth is represented by a debt, that the dead thing has been taken and made to look alive again, makes no difference to the loss. It has been done, of course, in order that those who lent the money may have security. They get their interest and ultimately their capital back. But that is not an additional burden on the community. This is proved by the fact that if this country repudiated its internal debt, or ceased to pay interest, or paid interest at only half rates, it would be no better off. It would have gained certain indirect advantages, shortly to be discussed, but on the main issue it would be exactly as it was before repudiation took place. Of course, the national credit would have been destroyed and no one would be prepared to lend money again to such a country except on usurious terms. In short, the nation would have been extremely dishonest. But the point is that the direct burden of loss is not increased by payment of interest on debt and the taxation it entails, and is not diminished by ceasing to pay, and reducing taxation. Certain classes, of course, would gain, and certain would lose, by repudiation. The taxpayer would gain, the holder of war loans would lose. If a man were in the position that he paid in taxes over the period of debt redemption exactly what he received in war loan interest and repayment, he would be precisely where he is now. And the country as a whole, the government and the people considered as one unit, is in the position of that man. The loss is the destruction of 5,000 million pounds' worth of wealth, not the payment of interest. And although interest on that sum is now paid in pounds that represent more purchasing power than did the pounds which were originally spent, the direct loss is not increased thereby. Because what the taxpayer loses by paying money that has appreciated in value, the bondholder gains by receiving it. Thus, changes in the value of money affect the national debt by altering the distribution of wealth as between taxpayers and bondholders, but do not affect the total of the country's loss. The result of such changes is of importance because of the relative uses to which taxpayer and bondholder put their money, and this point applies to the whole question of transfer from one set of persons to the other. If taxpayers as a whole are poorer than bondholders as a whole, the payment of interest on war debt makes the distribution of wealth more uneven than it would otherwise be. This is injurious to the real wealth of the community. Moreover, if the bondholder as a class puts money to less productive uses than the taxpayer as a class, the process of transfer does decrease the total resources of the nation, although the fact of transfer does not do so. Since the reserves of public companies and the profits of private business are subject to income tax, this sort of injury does in fact arise, for money is taken from productive uses and paid over to people who may spend rather than save it. Thus though no direct burden is imposed on the country as a whole by the service of the debt, there is an indirect burden. This is increased by the fact that high rates of taxation tend to reduce people's desire to work and save, and hence tend to check production. If people know that a large proportion of the income which they earn will be taken by the government they will be less eager to work and save in order to add to that income. The greater the proportion taken, the greater the check to productive effort. Smaller production means higher prices, and smaller savings mean less and dearer capital for industry. Consequently the heavy rate of taxation which is necessary to meet its debt obligations is a real burden to the country, and if the real rate of taxation is increased while the nominal rate remains the same (as is the case when prices fall), this indirect burden is increased. It is lightened as debt is paid off or as the interest to be paid upon it is reduced by conversion. Thus though repayment of debt cannot make good the loss that has been suffered, it can and does lighten the burden of taxation, and consequently reduces the check to work and saving which that burden involves.

Moreover, as debt is repaid, the rate of interest on the remainder tends to decline. The main reason for this is, of course, that repayment of debt is a sign, or is taken as a sign, that the finances of the country are in a healthy condition, that revenue exceeds expenditure, and consequently that that country is a good one in which to have money invested. Another subsidiary reason for the tendency of interest rates to fall during a period of debt repayment is that, particularly in this country, large numbers of people are bound by various legal instruments such as marriage settlements, to invest their capital in ‘ trustee securities.’ British government stocks form the highest class of this kind of security, and naturally people like to have some of their capital in them. As the total amount of these securities diminishes, competition to invest in them increases, the price of stock goes up, the yield down, until the government can probably convert their debt into a stock bearing a lower rate of interest. This was a feature of British finance in the latter half of the nineteenth century. The rate of interest on government stocks grew progressively less until Goschen in 1888 was able to convert the nation's funded debt into a stock bearing interest at the rate of only $2\frac{1}{2}$ per cent. per annum, and even then the stock stood at a high premium.

Yet another weighty reason for reducing debt is that should another emergency arise which necessitates further borrowing, the state will be able to obtain its loans more cheaply if it has not already pledged a large part of the taxable capacity of its citizens for the repayment of existing debt. But whether repayment should be accomplished quickly or over a long series of years is a matter of debate. It may be better to impose a special levy in one or a series of years, such as will enable a great part of the debt to be repaid, with the result that high rates of taxation and the check to saving are not prolonged into the future. On the other hand, it may be thought that annual taxation, even at a high rate, is less injurious to industry than the more drastic method. But, whichever course is adopted, this fact remains the same. By repaying debt all that happens is that money is taken from the taxpayer and given to the bondholder. Past losses are not made good nor present wealth increased. Prospective wealth, however, through the encouragement to industry which will result from lower rates of taxation is increased.

EXTERNAL DEBT

So much for internal debt. An external debt is its opposite. The burden is not the original loss of wealth, but payment of interest and repayment of capital. When Great Britain borrowed 1,000 million pounds from the United States and blew it off into the air it suffered no immediate loss. The money formed no part of Great Britain's wealth. It was not withdrawn from British industry. Its destruction did not deplete British capital. The loss was not felt by this country until she started to pay interest and sinking fund. Then her real wealth was diminished. Each year that 30 million pounds and more are sent across the Atlantic the resources in this country are lessened by that amount. Payment of interest and repayment of capital is the real burden of external debt. It is continuous. When a private citizen loses his own money, he feels the loss once and for all. The tooth is pulled out. In the case of Great Britain's debt to America, it goes on aching. And it will continue to ache until 1984. The only way to stop it is to repay the capital, and that means losing another tooth from a rather depleted set.

There is another disagreeable feature of external debt. Interest must be paid and capital refunded abroad, and in a foreign currency. The American debt is paid, not in sterling in London, but in dollars in New York. Those dollars must be bought, and questions of exchange come in.[1]

[1] Since payment of the debt is made in dollars, the number of pounds to be paid varies with the dollar-sterling exchange. So long as the movements of this exchange correspond to movements of the relative purchasing power of money in Great Britain and America, this fact is of no real consequence. For if prices rise in this country, and the pound falls in terms of dollars, although a greater number of pounds have to be spent on the service of the debt, each pound that we take from the taxpayer is worth less, and consequently the real burden of taxation is not increased. But so long as the exchange is not in equilibrium with relative price movements, and for short periods and with changing price levels this is often the case, the country stands to lose or gain on the exchange transactions. At the moment (December 1931) all payments of war debts are suspended under the Hoover moratorium plan. Were this not so, with a depreciated pound which has, however, maintained its internal purchasing power, the burden of the external debt would be increased.

HOW DEBT IS HELD

The actual holder of any national debt (except floating debt – a term which will be described in the following chapter) can hold it in three different ways. It may be inscribed stock or registered stock or bearer bonds. The holder of inscribed stock has his name written in the books of the Bank of England. This is his title. He holds no document of title. If he sells and wants to transfer to his purchaser, he either attends personally at the Bank, where he must be identified by some person known to the Bank, his London banker, or more usually his London stockbroker: his name is struck out and that of the new holder inscribed. Or, what more usually happens, he appoints an agent to carry through the transaction. The agent is called his attorney, and the document appointing him a power of attorney. It must be signed by him in the presence of a witness. The attorney must be known to the Bank, and therefore again must be either a London banker or stockbroker, usually the latter. The disadvantage of this method of holding is that the owner has to go to the Bank personally, which is very inconvenient if he lives out of London, and ordinarily employs a provincial broker, as sales of inscribed stock can only be made through a London stockbroker. Consols are mostly inscribed. Dividends are paid by sending the holder a warrant by post, which he can cash like a cheque, or, if he prefers, they are paid direct to his bank.

In registered stock the holder's name is similarly written in the Bank's register, but he also holds a stock certificate, made out in his name. His certificate is his document of title; but when he sells he must do more than hand this certificate to the buyer. He must transfer the stock to him by an ordinary transfer deed, signed in the presence of a witness. The buyer sends certificate and transfer to the Bank, and they send him a new certificate in his own name. This form of holding, the common form of most limited companies, was introduced for Consols in 1911. It is popular. The holder need not attend at the Bank, nor employ a London stockbroker, and everyone understands it. It should be noted also that it is a safe system. Should a certificate be stolen, the thief cannot deal with it without forgery, which since the true owner's signature is known to the Bank, should be easily detected. Again, if a holder lose his certificate, he does not lose his stock. He can get a new one by proving his loss to the Bank and indemnifying them against a double claim. Dividends are paid in the same manner as on inscribed stock.

The third form of holding is a bearer bond. This can be passed from hand to hand like a five-pound note. The bond constitutes the only title of the holder. Holders are not registered at the Bank. Attached to the bond are coupons for interest payments, and these, when dividends fall due, are cut off and either presented to the Bank or passed through the holder's own bank. Bearer securities are convenient, but risky. If lost, they cannot be replaced : if stolen, the thief can easily find a market, and if the buyer takes in good faith and for value he gets a good title. They are used much more in other countries than in Great Britain.

In technical terms, inscribed stock is said to be transferable in the Bank's books, register stocked transferable by deed and bearer bonds transferable by delivery.

HOW DEBT IS CREATED

The House of Commons alone can authorise borrowing. The authority may be a continuing one, as it is now under the War Loan Acts, in the case of loans raised to repay existing obligations. Or it may be special, as it was in the case of Consols issued before the war. Some authority from the House of Commons there must be.[1] For an addition to the national debt a resolution is introduced in Committee of Ways and Means, authorising the loan. This passes committee and report, and is then embodied in a special act, or in the next Consolidated Fund Act or Appropriation Act. However, the Treasury are allowed to issue the loan as soon as the resolution has passed Committee of Ways and Means, without waiting for the act : but the act must have passed before the first payment of interest is made on the new stock. Accordingly the Treasury issue a warrant to the Bank, who create the stock by entries in their books, either inscribed or registered, or print bearer bonds. In practice, preparations for the issue were made prior to the passage of the resolution by the Committee of Ways and Means, so that immediately the resolution had been agreed to by the committee a prospectus inviting subscriptions could be issued. The prospectus is important, for it contains the terms upon which lenders advance money, and the government is as much bound by every word of it as is a

[1] The procedure outlined used to be the ordinary method of procedure before the war. Whether the House of Commons will ever be able to wrest back from the Treasury the authority delegated to that department during the war is doubtful.

board of directors. Its terms are settled between the Treasury and the Bank : they include price of issue, rate of interest, date and terms of repayment if there are any, and other essential conditions. Subscribers apply for stock in the ordinary way, paying a deposit to the Bank. If the loan is over-subscribed, small applicants usually get an allotment in full, large ones a proportionate amount. They all pay over the balance, the Bank enters their name in its books or issues a certificate or bond as the case may be, and the transaction is over. The Bank pays straight into the Consolidated Fund all amounts received.

On the willingness or otherwise of investors to lend their money to the government depends the success or failure of the loan, hence the importance of the prospectus in which the terms on which the Treasury proposes to borrow the money are set out at length. These conditions must be sufficiently attractive to ensure the full amount of the loan being subscribed, yet not such as would unduly cheapen government credit in the market or depress existing securities below a certain level. The principal consideration in the minds both of the Treasury and the investing public must be the probable relation between money values now and money values in the future, so far as human prescience can foretell them. In the Treasury's answer to the problem, as set out in the prospectus, lies the reason for the varying nature of the national debt. This debt has already been classified into two fundamental divisions, external and internal, but each of these divisions can be sub-divided into three classes in which the time of repayment is the distinguishing factor. When times are prosperous, money cheap and no great national crisis in sight, the Treasury will succeed in borrowing money with no fixed date for repayment. In technical language such a contract is called a perpetual annuity, and government debt of this nature is spoken of as funded. The greater part of Britain's permanent debt before the war was of this kind. At the other end of the scale, the government requires money to carry on its day-to-day work, for it may be remembered that the revenue does not flow into the Exchequer as a regular placid stream ; it is for nearly nine months merely a tiny driblet, only swollen into a great torrent during the concluding three months of the financial year. For this day-to-day expenditure the Treasury, by the Appropriation Act, is given power to borrow on the credit of the lump sum voted by Parliament for the service of the year, and all money so borrowed must be repaid within the year. Money borrowed in this way is known as short-term debt or floating debt, and formed the second portion of the national debt before the war. But between these two classes there now lies a third. The terms on which the government can borrow are, as has already been explained, dependent on the result of a compromise between the views taken by the investor and the Treasury respectively as to the probable future trend of money values. In times of stress, and above all in times of war, the value of money usually falls very sharply. In such a time the amount of currency in the country is likely to be increased, as happened during the last war (*see* Chapter IX.). Prices then rise, and the real value the investor receives in interest on the capital he has lent to the government falls. If he foresees this state of affairs, and during a war he will certainly foresee it, the investor stands out either for a very high rate of interest or for repayment of his capital by a certain date, or for a mixture of both. The result is the creation of a debt redeemable at a fixed date, which at its inception may be so distant as to resemble funded debt, but which, as that term slowly matures, gradually approximates to floating debt, until at length the two are indistinguishable. The three main sub-classifications of debt, it may be repeated, are funded, redeemable or intermediate, and floating. The elements comprising each of these classes will be considered in detail in the next chapter.

CHAPTER XI

THE NATIONAL DEBT

FUNDED DEBT

On 31st March, 1931, the total funded debt of the United Kingdom, as set out in the Finance Accounts for the year, was over 1,425 million pounds. Of this, some 312 millions represents the pre-war funded debt, the remainder the first attempts to fund the vast debt which during the war had to be incurred on short-term loans. In the last chapter it was stated that the distinguishing feature of funded debt was that no time is fixed for repayment ; that statement requires amplification. When issuing a funded loan, the Treasury in fact guarantees that for every £100 nominal of stock the investor or his heirs shall receive a certain sum each quarter for the remainder of time. The price of the £100 'nominal' of stock is fixed in the prospectus, or may be tendered for, and will vary, of course, with the credit of the government and the general state of the money market. The creditor cannot claim to be repaid the capital he has advanced, but there is usually in the terms a provision under which the Treasury may at *their* option, on or after a fixed date and after notice given, pay off the loan at par. For instance, since 1923 the government could, if they desired, at three months' notice pay off the holders of Consols, and they will have the same option on 4 per cent. Consols after 1st February, 1957, and on 3½ per cent. Conversion after 1st April, 1961. The three loans mentioned form the greater part of the funded debt of the country. There are still 2 millions odd of the 2¾ per cent. created in 1884, and 21 millions of the 2½ per cent. of the same date, but the bulk of the pre-war debt was in the form of 2½ per cent. Consols, the result of Goschen's great conversion in 1888, when the long-term debt of the country was put on a 2½ per cent. basis. There are still 276 millions of this outstanding (31st March, 1931). The original prospectus of the 3½ per cent. loan, the first effort to fund a part of the war debt, appeared on 26th April, 1921, and was an attempt to convert into funded debt 632 millions of short-term bonds which matured between the years 1921 and 1925. The offer was a generous one, for the government had, almost at any cost, to rid itself of some of the vast mass of short-term debt which threatened to engulf the finance of the country. In 1921 however trade had slumped, and even in good times taxation could not have provided so gigantic a capital sum even when spread over five years, nor could the Treasury raise the money by three months bills, since the floating debt then stood at the staggering sum of 1,300 millions. In the event, the bulk of the debt was successfully funded, though at the expense of a large increase in the nominal capital liability and of a small addition to the annual interest charge.

As the Chancellor could not compel the bondholders to convert he had to persuade them not to demand repayment in cash by making them an offer which they would accept. What was this offer? It was an exchange which gave them over 5½ per cent. for forty years.[1] Those terms to-day seem extraordinarily high. Yet they were wise terms, for they succeeded in inducing most of the bondholders to convert. First, then, it was good policy to make certain of the bondholders accepting the terms by making them very favourable. Second, they had to be offered some time ahead, that is some time before repayment was due, for otherwise the government might have been squeezed. Hence the government could not wait and take advantage of the fall of interest which everyone knew would occur. Third, if they had had actually to find the 632 millions, it would have cost them more than 5½ per cent. Fourth, the debt would be off their minds till 1961, and even then repayment was only at the option of the government. It could not be demanded, and therefore would not always be hanging over the Treasury's head. Those were sound and prudent reasons. But there is a further explanation of the seemingly extravagant terms, not generally realised. The Conversion Loan of 1921 was the first great conversion of war debt. It would not be the last. Huge blocks of war debt were falling due in the next few years. All of these had to be converted. The terms of subsequent conversions had to be progressively worse for the investor. If they were not, he would wait and not convert. He must know that if he did not take the government's offer he would get less next time. Therefore the first offer had to be very high, to allow of this scaling down.

That is made clearer by the recollection of what

[1] For each £100 of National War Bonds holders were offered from £160 to £163 (varying with the date of repayment of the bond) of 3½ per cent. Conversion Loan 1961. This gave them interest from £5 12s. to £5 14s. per cent.

happened at the beginning of the war. Then the process was reversed. Investors were likely to hold back because interest would rise. That was met by allowing those who subscribed to an early loan at a low rate to exchange into a later one at a higher. There was therefore no inducement to hold back. After the war investors were likely to refrain from converting, if they thought they would get better terms later. It was essential that this should not be so. It would have jeopardised all future conversions. The Chancellor of the Exchequer in 1921 had in mind not only the immediate operation, but a whole series of them, reaching out to 1949. He had to pitch his terms so high, that each subsequent offer might be progressively lower, and yet not so bad that the investor would refuse it. This demanded an ample margin.

In addition to the high rate of interest another attraction was offered. The government undertook that at the end of any half-year during which the average price of the loan was under 90 they would set aside an amount equal to 1 per cent. of the amount of the loan outstanding with which in the course of the next half-year to purchase stock and cancel it. The effects of this special sinking fund are, of course, to prevent depreciation of the stock, and will be more opportunely discussed when the subject of sinking funds is reached.

There were further issues of 3½ per cent. stock during the year 1925 at a price to be tendered for, not lower than £77 10*s.* 0*d.* per 100 nominal. In fact, the government got nearly 1*s.* per £100 more than the minimum price. The 1925 issue was to rank *pari passu* with that of 1921. There were nearly 770 millions of this loan outstanding at 31st

March, 1931. In December 1926 the Treasury issued a prospectus of a new loan, the 4 per cent. Consols. This could be subscribed for in cash at £85 per £100 nominal, or certain bonds could be tendered for conversion at corresponding rates. The loan was redeemable at the option of the government at par after 1st February, 1957, and it also had a special sinking fund attached to it. For ten years, between 1st May, 1927, and 30th April, 1937, the government undertook to spend 10 millions a year in purchasing stock from the market, provided that the price was under par. On 31st March, 1931, there were about 342 millions of this stock outstanding. The last item of irredeemable debt consists of the government's debts to the Banks of England and Ireland (Scotland has no central bank). That to the former amounts to some 11 millions, to the latter, two – in all, some 13 or 14 millions.

REDEEMABLE OR INTERMEDIATE DEBT

The second class of debt that has now to be examined is redeemable or intermediate debt, because, though, strictly speaking, floating debt, and appearing as such in the finance accounts, this class has certain definite, well-defined characteristics, and is more conveniently discussed apart from the floating debt proper. The essential difference between funded and redeemable debt lies in the creditor's right, in the latter case, to be repaid on a specified date. The debtor may, or may not, have a right to pay off the money at an earlier date, but the essential feature of redeemable debt is that on some definite day the holder can call for his money.

As the date of maturity draws near, it is obvious that this type of debt tends to merge into the type of floating debt proper ; indeed, the distinction between certain debt of the redeemable type and Treasury bills is one largely of time. On the whole, however, it is fair to say that unfunded debt which lies outside the scope of the weekly return of floating debt, a copy of which is given on p. 183, can be included in the intermediate type. It has already been explained that when a war cannot be paid for out of revenue, there is little prospect of its being financed by an immediate increase in the permanent funded debt of the country concerned. That will come later, but for its immediate necessities a country will have to depend on increasing its redeemable, or, worse still, its floating debt. It is, therefore, in this category of ' intermediate redeemable debt ' that a large war increase would naturally be expected. A closer study, in fact, will reveal that as it exists to-day this class of debt was practically created during the war.

Since then this type of debt ought slowly to have disappeared. Unfortunately, the size of its constantly maturing obligations, and the disturbances and perils through which the country has passed since the Armistice, have prevented the Treasury from launching a long series of conversion operations on a scale at all commensurate with the magnitude of the short-term debts maturing. The result is that the category of debt now under consideration covers numerous loans of an extremely miscellaneous nature, many of which have come into existence to enable former loans of much the same character to be paid off. Borrowing short to meet maturing obligations, in the hope that, when the new loan in its turn reaches maturity, conditions will enable the debtor to fund the debt, is a policy which can only be regarded with suspicion as unworthy of the financial status of this country, and excusable only by reason of the magnitude of the sums involved and the general difficulties of the post-war period. These difficulties, however, emphasise the importance of financial stability, for until investors are reasonably assured of stable conditions, large-scale conversions of short-term debt are not possible. But until such conversions have taken place the nation will receive no substantial relief from the crushing burden of the interest payments on its debts, amounting in the year ended 31st March, 1931, to nearly 292 million pounds.

There is no doubt, however, that during the war this type of loan suited both the investor and the government better than the funded type. The investor, however patriotic (and the British war record is a fine one), could not have been expected to lock up what was perhaps the bulk of his fortune in an irredeemable stock, which paid the then current rate of interest ; for as money got scarcer interest was sure to rise and he would suffer a heavy capital loss when he had to sell. The government, too, had it borrowed on irredeemable stock, might have saddled the country for all time with the high war rates of interest. The four great war loans, those of 1914, 1915, 1917 and the Victory Loan of 1919, were attempts to borrow for as long a period as possible at as low a rate of interest as possible. To do this successfully three principles had to be observed. First, the terms had to be progressively better. That was a necessity. In fact, interest rose from over 4 per cent. in 1914 to a rate between

£5 6*s.* 8*d.* and £5 11*s.* 4*d.* per cent. in 1917.[1] Secondly, earlier subscribers must be allowed to share the profit of later issues, otherwise they would hold back in the hope of more favourable terms. Thirdly, the public must be given what they want and treated fairly. All these rules were followed. Successive loans offered various attractions to induce lenders to subscribe. Many were offered at a premium. Others were issued below par and made redeemable by annual drawings. This gave a speculative interest to the investment, as such stock as was drawn at an early date brought a handsome bonus on repayment. Another attractive feature was the fact that certain loans were accepted at par in payment of death-duties. One loan was offered free of income tax. This gave the investor a certain return not subject to tax increases. Again, in order that people should not hold back from earlier loans, in the hope that better terms might be obtained as the war went on and the rate of interest rose, the right was given to holders to convert their holdings of earlier loans into new issues on favourable terms. Finally, certain loans had substantial sinking funds attached to them to be used in buying up and cancelling stock. This steadied the capital value of such loans. When the huge sums that were needed for financing the war are borne in mind, it must be admitted that these arrangements were undoubtedly successful. On the whole the Treasury borrowed cheaply, and British credit stood the strain in a manner which was astounding.

[1] Interest on temporary advances rose substantially higher.

TERMINABLE ANNUITIES

It has been stated that before the war 'redeemable or intermediate debt' was almost unknown. Almost, but not quite, for, in fact, two varieties of this nature were in existence. The oldest of these methods of raising money, dating as it does from the Napoleonic Wars, is the terminable annuity.

The general characteristics of this form of borrowing are that the lender advances a capital sum to the government, and gets in return an annual sum paid over a period of years, of an amount which will pay interest and an instalment of capital, so that at the end of the period the total capital is repaid. In other words, these yearly payments cover interest and sinking fund. It is a useful way of borrowing money and spreading the cost of repayment over several years.

Two or three different sorts of terminable annuities appear in the finance accounts. The first, a small sinking fund annuity, is so much akin to the sinking fund proper that it will be dealt with under that head. Another representing a capital liability of nearly 12 millions is the result of sales to the public of annuities for life or terms of years. Anyone can buy an annuity from the office of the Commissioners for the National Debt in Old Jewry, and the terms are regulated by the provisions of the Government Annuities Act, 1929, which is an act consolidating and harmonising a long series of acts of Parliament on this subject.

The government's commitments to annuitants, however, are hardly a liability, for the Commissioners buy government stock with the purchase price of the annuity and cancel it, and the terms given to the annuitant are calculated on the market price of government stock. In fact the government gets more favourable terms than those obtained by leading insurance offices. Life annuities are charged on the Consolidated Fund.

Another kind of annuity found in the accounts, which appears among the capital liabilities of the state but not as a part of the national debt, is in the form of annuities authorised by statute to be charged on the votes of various departments.

The four and a quarter millions which the Anglo-Persian Oil shares cost were so raised. Capital for light railways is so obtained. The whole of the cost of telegraph and telephone construction is financed by this method. These last annuities are charged on the Post Office vote and appear in the estimates: the capital sum is received by the Post Office and spent on works. In 1930–1, 11 millions of annuities charged on this vote were created under the Post Office and Telegraph (Money) Act, 1928. These terminable annuities are not sold in the open market. Most are bought by the National Debt Commissioners, who have large sums to invest, including savings bank deposits. The Commissioners, of course, separate and invest such part of each annual receipt as represents capital. On 31st March, 1931, the nation's liability on the score of these terminable annuities was 7,582 millions. The government also lends money on this system. For instance the Ministry of Agriculture advance moneys to landowners for drainage or improvements, taking a thirty-year charge.

The terminable annuities described have all been of the nature of internal debt, but a very large liability of this kind is the debt to America, which in 1923 was nominally funded but really transformed into a terminable annuity amounting in all to 930 million pounds. Originally the bulk of this money was borrowed as floating debt – that is, money repayable at call. This was the original character of the large advances the United States made to Great Britain after April 1917 when they entered the war. And from that year onwards a regular weekly quota of 15 million dollars three-month Treasury Bills were placed on the New York market. The rest of the debt was borrowed on short-dated loans, the terms of which varied from five years downwards. There were in addition large sums owing for armaments and food, secured by various means. Some indebtedness was repaid by 1923: but when Mr. Stanley Baldwin, then Chancellor of the Exchequer, and the Governor of the Bank of England met the American authorities in January of that year, the total with accrued interest was agreed at 4,600 million dollars. Under the Funding Agreement of 18th and 19th June, 1923, Great Britain undertook to pay interest on that amount half-yearly, starting from 15th December, 1922, at the rate of 3 per cent. for the first ten years and thereafter at 3½ per cent. till 1984. The principal is repayable by yearly instalments, beginning with 23 million dollars in 1923 and rising to 175 million dollars in 1984. There is the right to repay earlier, on giving short notice.

In June 1931 payment of war debts was suspended for one year at the suggestion of Mr. Hoover, President of the United States of America.

EXCHEQUER BONDS

The other pre-war form of redeemable debt were Exchequer Bonds. They were an excellent method of raising money for a particular emergency, and avoided a permanent increase of the national debt. To be fully effective, however, annual drawings of the bonds were essential ; in other words, a certain proportion of capital should be repaid each year. This condition was not always fulfilled in the case of Exchequer Bonds, but when any large sum is borrowed without some such safeguard, the cash can probably no more be raised at the time of the maturity of the bonds than it would have been at the original time of borrowing. The result, therefore, must be either fresh redeemable borrowing or an increase of the permanent debt. On the other hand, if a certain amount of capital is paid off each year, Exchequer Bonds tend to assimilate to the conditions of a terminable annuity. Some £362,000 of Exchequer Bonds issued under the Capital Expenditure (Money) Act, 1904, for the purposes of the Naval Works Act were outstanding on 31st March, 1931, and appear in the finance accounts of the year on the same footing as terminable annuities chargeable on the votes of a department. Exchequer Bonds were one of the methods employed in financing the Boer War, and again served this purpose in the early stages of the Great War.

The first issue was made in March 1915. These bonds were repayable in five years and sold by tender, a process which will be described in connection with Treasury Bills. On and after December 1915 Exchequer Bonds at 5 per cent. were on sale daily, this being the then method of raising short loans, and a very successful method too. These and later bonds could, like some war loan issues, be used to pay not only death-duties, but excess profits duty and munitions levy. All Exchequer Bonds were discontinued in 1917 until after the war, when a further issue was made. Fifteen millions of this latter issue were paid off in the year ended 31st March, 1930, and there are none now outstanding.

NATIONAL WAR BONDS

Exchequer Bonds are the link between pre-war and war finance in the sphere of redeemable debt. Their immediate successors were National War Bonds, the change being an intentional change of name. It was felt that a National War Bond would appeal to an investor, to whom the expression Exchequer Bond was recondite and alarming. They were on sale daily, not only at the Bank of England, but at all banks. The amount raised by National War Bonds was immense, and ultimately reached over 1,700 millions. The bonds were redeemed at various dates up to 1929, and none are now outstanding.

WAR EXPENDITURE CERTIFICATES

War Expenditure Certificates were issued for about six months after June 1916, at a rate of interest varying with the bank rate. They were never popular, and soon dropped. They are interesting only as an example of the experiments that have to be made when money is required in hitherto undreamed-of amounts. War Expenditure Certificates failed to tickle the investor's fancy.

WAR SAVINGS CERTIFICATES

War Savings Certificates had a very different history. They were novel, ingenious and successful. They were designed to attract small savings and to give the humble investor a certain return without capital loss, and they accomplished both objects. For a payment of 15*s*. 6*d*. a purchaser got the right to receive £1 at the end of five years. But he could draw his money out earlier if he wanted it, 15*s*. 6*d*. during the first year, 15*s*. 9*d*. at the end of one year, and an additional 1*d*. for each succeeding month. It is therefore money at call. If not withdrawn, his certificate continues to earn interest up to ten years. He is given a book, like his post office savings bank book, which is so well understood, and in this payments and withdrawals are entered. At first War Savings Certificates were on sale at any Money Order Office of the Post Office, but later at banks also. No income tax is payable on interest, but no one is allowed to hold more certificates than will give him £500 on repayment. Their name was changed to National Savings Certificates in 1920, and the price raised to 16*s*. on 1st April, 1922.

The nation's liability under this head increased by some 13 millions during the year ended 31st March, 1931. It now stands at over 372 million pounds. So much for war and immediate post-war finance. The next item arose after the war, but as a consequence of war conditions.

TREASURY BONDS

Treasury Bonds were started in 1920, and have been issued occasionally since. Originally they were issued for periods of fifteen years, with an option both to government and holder to effect repayment at the end of any year after the first five : then they were to run for ten years certain, while the last issue, made in 1930–1, was to run for three years certain, with the possibility of an extension to five. Issued with the object of reducing the colossal figures of the floating debt, Treasury Bonds have proved successful in that there were, at 31st March, 1931, over 600 millions of them in existence. At the same time they are definitely of the nature of short-term debt, and the continuous maturity of large blocks of this sort of debt is a perpetual menace to the budgetary position of the country, while the equally perpetual issue of short-term bonds savours of a much lower order of finance than that with which Great Britain is usually associated. To illustrate the difficulties of having these bonds maturing year after year it is only necessary to look at the finance accounts for the last two years. In the year ended 31st March, 1930, 26 millions of these bonds were created to mature between 1932 and 1934, about 45 millions were paid off, 9 millions converted into funded debt, and 109 millions into a redeemable debt with at least fourteen years to run. There was thus a net reduction on the year of 138 millions of Treasury Bonds, though be it noted only the 9 millions funded and the 45 millions paid off were really disposed of. Then in the next year, ending 31st March, 1931, 105 millions of Treasury Bonds were created by cash subscriptions to mature between the years 1934 and 1936, and only about 40 millions paid off, so that an increase actually took place amounting to about 65 million pounds net.

That concludes the description of debt of all classes, except floating debt. It will be noticed that peace finance was almost entirely effected by funded loans, war finance by redeemable ones. It is safe to prophesy that funded debt will again become the ordinary method. The 3½ per cent. Conversion Loan of 1921 and the 4 per cent. Consols of 1926 are funded, for though the government can redeem them, a holder has never any right to call for his capital. Thus a return to peace conditions has been started, but the road is long and arduous. A glance at the table given at the end of this chapter will show the tremendous weight of debt maturing in the course of the next few years. The Treasury has uphill work in front of it, and its task is made none the easier from having to be performed in a world which financially is topsy-turvy.

TABLE OF DATES ON WHICH REDEEMABLE DEBT (APART FROM FLOATING DEBT) WILL MATURE.

Latest date of maturity	*Amount in £ (to nearest million)*	*Name of loan*
1932	116	4½% Treasury Bonds.
1932	1	4 % ,, ,,
1933	64	4 % ,, ,,
1934	65	4½% ,, ,,
1934	140	4½% ,, ,,
1935	115	5 % ,, ,,
1936	105	4 % ,, ,,
1944	316	4½% Conversion Loan.
1945	13	4½% War ,,
1947	2,087	5 % War ,,
Total	3,022	

In the next sixteen years, 3,022 millions of debt matures, i.e. on an average 183 millions must be converted, paid off or re-borrowed on short loan terms for each of the next sixteen years.

Latest date of maturity	*Amount in £ (to nearest million)*	*Name of loan*
1964	323	5% Conversion Loan.
1990	375	4% Funding ,,

The table takes no account of Victory Bonds, which are repayable by annual drawings.

CHAPTER XII

FLOATING DEBT

THE term floating debt ought strictly to be applied to all unfunded obligations. In the last chapter, however, a number of such liabilities were dealt with, and, though the line is admittedly hard to draw, the term floating debt in this chapter is confined to money borrowed for a short time, not by means of a loan in which the public invest their savings, but by a bill of exchange or bank overdraft or similar means. Before the war short-time borrowing was, with a very small exception, confined to occasions when payments out of the Consolidated Fund were heavier than revenue receipts. It was therefore not really a part of our national debt, but was used to fill a temporary gap between expenditure and income. Such temporary borrowing there must always be, for the stream of payments into and out of the Consolidated Fund never exactly coincide, and the authority to anticipate revenue in this way is given in each Consolidated Fund Act and Appropriation Act. But at present the floating debt is not confined to advances of this temporary nature. During the war very large sums were borrowed on short-term loans, and much of this borrowing has been continuously renewed, and is still outstanding. Fresh issues have also been made to meet maturing liabilities. The result is that floating debt is now very large, a legacy of war, and quite a substantial part of the nation's liabilities.

The following statement has been extracted from the financial columns of *The Times* for Wednesday, 9th December, 1931 :

(000's omitted)

Floating Debt	Dec. 5, 1931	Nov. 28, 1931	Dec. 6, 1930
Ways and Means Advances :—	£	£	£
By Bank of England ..	2,500	—	16,250
By Public Departments ..	50,600	32,050	31,100
Treasury Bills outstanding	667,600	637,770	700,295
Total	720,700	669,820	747,645

That statement, properly understood, contains the whole history of floating debt, and is worthy of a close examination.

The statement shows the current floating debt in the first column, that of the previous week in the second, and that of a year ago in the third, and therefore increases or decreases are seen at a glance. That is simple : but what is the meaning of the elements of which that debt is made up, and who settles the amount of each item ? At four o'clock every afternoon the Treasury balance the Consolidated Fund which, it may be remembered, is the same as the Exchequer Account kept at the Bank of England. If taxes have been coming in slowly, or if the departments have asked the Paymaster-General to pay heavy bills, or still more if there is due one of the big dividends on war loan, the government's balance may run low or the account be in danger of being overdrawn. The

Treasury therefore have to feed it. This they can do from three sources: Advances from Public Departments, Ways and Means Advances from the Bank of England, and Treasury Bills. These three sources combined make up our floating debt.

ADVANCES FROM PUBLIC DEPARTMENTS

The Treasury look round and see which departments have credit balances. The National Debt Commissioners may have savings bank money waiting for investment; the Paymaster-General holds cash which the spending departments may not want at once; the Public Trustee may have funds in hand; or there may be some other source available. The Treasury therefore borrow temporarily from these accounts. All these balances are of course kept at the Bank of England, so the money is merely transferred. During the war very large advances were obtained from the departments in this way. Some of these have been repaid, but a considerable part has been continuously renewed, and still contributes to the increased volume of the floating debt. Interest is limited by statute to 5 per cent., and at present is less. The Paymaster-General, however, gets no interest. He does not want it. All he needs is money to pay the nation's bills, and that he has already. The arrangement is convenient for all the parties concerned. The state does not want to keep money unnecessarily locked up, while the departments, owing to the liquid nature of the asset they have obtained, can lay their hands on the cash the moment it is required. Borrowing of this nature is authorised by the Consolidated Fund and Appropriation Acts.

WAYS AND MEANS ADVANCES FROM THE BANK OF ENGLAND

If the amount that can be obtained from the departments' balances is insufficient to replenish the Consolidated Fund, the Treasury can borrow on Ways and Means Advances from the Bank of England. That is a roundabout expression for a bank overdraft. Under a provision which is inserted in all Consolidated Fund or Appropriation Acts, the Treasury may ask the Bank to allow them to overdraw. When the Governor has agreed, the required sum is credited to the government. The Bank enter it in their books as an advance on government securities, which in fact it is, for the security is the taxpayer. Interest is paid at a rate agreed upon by the government and the Bank according to the Bank's official rate of discount: it must never exceed 5 per cent. Before the war Ways and Means Advances from the Bank were used as sparingly as possible, and had by statute to be repaid not later than the end of the quarter next succeeding that in which the advance had been made. During the war, however, these borrowings reached an enormous size, and were often renewed when the date of payment arrived. Now, they have again been reduced, and, as before the war, are only used to meet a temporary deficiency, and are strictly repaid.

TREASURY BILLS

It will be seen, however, that most of the floating debt is in Treasury Bills. A bill of exchange is a common mercantile method of raising money. It is a promise to pay the sum named upon the bill, at some specified future date, to the then holder of the bill. The drawer or holder borrows on the bill by selling it, for a bill is a negotiable instrument, and if the names upon it are good it can be readily sold.

To the late Mr. Walter Bagehot, a famous economist and at the time editor of the weekly paper called the *Economist*, belongs the credit of first suggesting that the Treasury should make use of this instrument of commerce. And a very cheap and convenient method of raising money it has proved. Technically known as a Treasury Bill, the process whereby these bills are put upon the market is simple. When in need of money, the Treasury send a warrant to the Bank authorising it to issue a specified amount of bills. This warrant requires to be countersigned by the Comptroller and Auditor-General, who has to see that there is parliamentary sanction for the issue. The Bank then does the rest of the work. A notice is published in the *London Gazette* setting out the amount of the bills, the day on which payment may be made for them,[1] and their date of repayment, and inviting tenders. At the present time issues are made every Friday of bills at three months. On the day specified for tendering, bankers, bill discounters and lenders of money generally send in their tenders stating how many bills they are willing to take, and how much they will give for the bill – that is, how much they will pay down in cash for the right to receive £100 in three months. This sum of course is less than £100, and the difference between the two is

[1] The existing practice is that bills may be paid for on any day of the week succeeding that in which the issue is made. Repayment, of course, is made on the corresponding day three months later.

what the government pay for the use of the money for three months.

The Treasury accept the cheapest tenders. If there are not enough offers at this rate to give them all the money required, they have to take a proportion of those that give worse terms. The result is announced in the Press, together with the average rate of tenders and the total amount of bills applied for and the amount allotted, which need not be the same as that offered.[1] Tenderers whose offers are accepted pay the amounts into the Bank of England on the day specified in the notice. Technically speaking, a three-months bill has been discounted. The difference between the sum paid to the Treasury and that which the Treasury will have to pay three months later is called the rate of discount.

Before the war, Treasury Bills were used in two ways. There was a permanent amount of about 14 million pounds always outstanding borrowed under the Treasury Bills Act, 1877 and other acts. These bills were regularly renewed, for the act of 1877 gave the Treasury power to renew bills as they matured, but, if they were not then renewed, the power lapsed and they could not subsequently be renewed. This amount of bills, therefore, really formed part of the national debt. Then after the South African war, when large sums had to be borrowed to meet war expenditure, the practice arose of inserting a section in the Consolidated Fund and Appropriation Acts, allowing the Treasury

[1] Extract from *The Times* of 5th December, 1931 : 'Applications for the £45,000,000 on offer declined from £53,195,000 to £49,745,000, and for the £44,570,000 allotted the average rate of discount worked out to £5 12*s*. 0.76*d*. per cent. per annum, against £5 11*s*. 6.27*d*. Tenders at £98 12*s*. for bills to be paid for on any day next week will receive allotment in full. Next Friday the amount of bills to be offered will be reduced to £40,000,000.'

to borrow by Treasury Bills or otherwise up to the amount of which the act authorised the issue. All bills issued under such authority must mature during the current financial year and could not be renewed under the act of 1877.

Under these two authorities 15 million pounds of Treasury Bills were outstanding on 1st August, 1914, and that was an average amount. At the present day there are about 668 million pounds outstanding, as will be seen from the extract from *The Times*.

The bills have changed in character and the power to issue them has changed in unison. Only a very small proportion of those now in circulation represent borrowing for temporary deficiencies. By far the greater part is due to the large sums borrowed on Treasury Bills during the war. Many of these bills have been renewed, while fresh issues have been made to meet other maturing liabilities. In this way they have become a large part of the national debt. Renewals and fresh issues of Treasury Bills are authorised by the War Loans Act, 1919, which empowers the Treasury to raise money to any extent wherewith to repay existing obligations. Since large blocks of redeemable debt are continually falling due for payment, the Treasury must have power to borrow money to meet these liabilities ; and by the War Loans Act they are enabled to renew all bills as they mature or to issue fresh ones as need arises. This in effect supersedes all other powers. It is probably essential that there should be this general authority to re-borrow, and, since the Treasury can only do so to the extent of maturing debt, total debt is not increased. But it is noticeable that the old control of the House of Commons over each individual issue of Treasury Bills has lapsed. It has granted a general authority, and it is a debatable point whether the time has not come to recall it. Treasury Bills issued under the terms of Consolidated Fund or Appropriation Acts are, however, subject to the same restrictions as to repayment as they were before the war.

During the war, when money had to be raised in blocks, the government at certain periods kept up a continuous sale of bills at a fixed rate of discount. Anyone could call at the Bank any day, pay his money and get his bill. This method survived the war in what was known as the ' tap rate.' After an issue, the Treasury offered any more bills which the public might want at a fixed rate of discount, always slightly below the rate at which the last Treasury Bills were allotted. They turned the ' tap ' on or off, as the national banking account required. During the war, when Treasury Bills carried a high rate of interest, they were held by the investing public as well as by big banks and discount houses. Now, however, they are taken up entirely by the latter, and the ' tap ' has been turned off, it is to be hoped for ever.

FLOATING DEBT, INFLATION AND DEFLATION

There is one aspect of floating debt which it is important to understand. The various forms of short-term borrowing which have just been described are not loans made out of the real savings of the public, they are advances made by the Bank of England, by government departments and by the joint stock banks. In varying degrees they all are creations of credit which add to the supply of money available. That is to say, their use tends to have an inflationary effect. The extent to which this is the case differs with the various forms of floating debt. Ways and Means Advances from the Bank are bank overdrafts, that is to say, new or invented money. But the total supply of money made available thereby is not limited to the amount of the Ways and Means Advances. It is that amount multiplied many times. The reason is as follows: the Bank lends, say, £100 to the government, the government spends the money, for the Paymaster-General pays it out to contractors or soldiers or local authorities or to anyone to whom the departments owe money. These persons pay the sums which they receive into their own banks, and therefore within a few days the greater part of the money flows back into the accounts which all these banks keep at the Bank of England. Now the joint stock banks treat the balances which they hold at the Bank of England as a cash reserve, on the basis of which they create credit, either by advances to traders, purchase of bills, or investments. It is their custom to keep their cash reserve (at the Bank and in their tills) at about 12 per cent. of their deposit liabilities.[1] Consequently when their reserves at the Bank of England are increased by the expenditure of the money created for the government they are able to increase the volume of their credit; and for every pound that their accounts at the Bank of England are increased, they are able to increase their credits by about eight pounds.

[1] As to the figure of 12 per cent., see Mr. J. M. Keynes' *Monetary Reform*, 1924, p. 178.

Consequently each pound of Ways and Means Advances is liable to cause an inflation, not of one pound only, but of nine. The position is different where money is borrowed from the Paymaster-General or from the National Debt Commissioners. In the case of the Paymaster-General no fresh money is created by the government, but a balance which would otherwise have been lying idle is used for current expenditure. Its use does not increase the amount of money, but it increases its rapidity of circulation. Until it is spent, money held by the Paymaster-General is money locked up. The borrowing of the money by the government merely transfers it to the deposits of the joint stock banks more quickly than it would otherwise have been transferred. It is probable that money borrowed from the Debt Commissioners would have been invested in some other way if it had not been lent to the government, therefore, in so far as such advances are an alternative use for money, there is no inflationary element in this form of borrowing.

And now as to Treasury Bills. At present these are taken up, for the most part, by the joint stock banks. The banks pay over the price of the bill to the government, and hold the Treasury Bill as security against the loan. So far the position is exactly the same as it would be had they bought trade bills. But Treasury Bills are an even more liquid asset than the ordinary commercial bill. The security is the best that can be offered, and they can be realised at any moment. Consequently the banks treat Treasury Bills almost as if they were cash, they use them as a backing for further credit. When therefore the government issue fresh Treasury Bills, they spend the money which the banks advance. The banks advance it on the basis of their cash reserves, but their lending capacity is not reduced as it would be by any other loan, for the Treasury Bill held against the advance is considered to be almost as good as cash.

Ways and Means Advances from the Bank are only used as need arises, but a large part of the national debt is now in the form of Treasury Bills, always outstanding and renewed as they fall due. But sometimes they are repaid, and from repayment important results follow. When the Treasury repays, it does so with money taken from the taxpayer or with money obtained from the public by a long-term loan.[1] In either case the money is drawn from the reserves of the banks at the Bank of England, it is transferred from ' Other Deposits ' to ' Public Deposits ' at the Bank of England, and as the Treasury Bills are repaid it is handed back to the banks again. So far therefore the reserves of the banks – the bases of credit – are the same as they were before. But the banks no longer hold the Treasury Bill, and therefore an asset against which credit could be created has been destroyed. In this way the repayment of Treasury Bills has a deflationary effect. But with regard to this point there is something to be said on the other side. The government is not the only issuer of bills of exchange, and it may be that the banks hold fewer commercial bills than they would otherwise do, as a result of their large holdings of Treasury Bills. First-class commercial bills are almost, though not quite, as liquid an asset as Treasury Bills, and it might be that if, by the repayment of Treasury Bills,

[1] If the Treasury is forced to repay Treasury Bills by unwillingness of the banks to renew their holdings, it may then have to find the money by borrowing from the Bank of England or from Public Departments.

the banks were enabled to hold a larger quantity of such first-class bills, very little deflation would result from the repayment. It must not be forgotten, however, that in a period of depression such as the present, any deflation, bringing in its train falling prices, is a serious hindrance to trade. The activities of trader and manufacturer are alike discouraged by the fact that goods are sold at a level of prices lower than that at which the manufacturer bought his raw material or the shopkeeper ought his stock.

But unless Treasury Bills are paid off, floating debt will never be reduced. It must be reduced. It is a danger and a weakness. No doubt money can be raised cheaply on Treasury Bills ; especially in times when, owing to trade slackness, manufacturers are not borrowing much, and the banks have plenty of money to lend to the government. But when trade is active, money gets scarce and the government has to pay more for its bills. Price is a fluctuating factor which, with so large an amount of bills outstanding, makes a very considerable difference to the annual cost of the debt, and therefore to the budget. But the real danger lies in having so large a floating debt hanging over the government's head when so many conversions are in front of them, and a great deal of money may be required in a hurry. The necessity of funding the war debt is the real reason why the floating debt must be reduced. But, whatever action is taken, due precaution must be observed, and the least possible damage must be done to trade. The time must be carefully chosen, and regard paid not only to the burden of the debt, but to the effect of a sudden deflation upon trade and commerce.

CONTINGENT LIABILITIES

Besides dead-weight debt, the state has undertaken certain guarantees and commitments under which it might possibly have to find money and thus add to the national debt. However, most of these, though large in amount, are small in burden. They fall roughly into three classes.

First of all are guarantees given to enable foreign powers to raise money in London. An example of this will be in everybody's mind: the reconstruction loan issued to Austria under the auspices of the League of Nations, of which this country guaranteed about one quarter. In the same class come certain similar guarantees which have been given for loans to Greece, Turkey, the Transvaal, Northern Ireland, the Soudan, Palestine and Tanganyika. In none of these cases is the obligation likely to be an actual one.

In the second class there is the government's guarantee of interest on, and some responsibility for the capital of Local Loans Stock. This is a fund formed to re-lend to the smaller local authorities who, if they had to borrow individually, would have to pay heavily for their money. The fund has been formed by the creation of Local Loans Stock, held partly by investors and partly by the National Debt Commissioners. The fund is managed by a special body called the Public Works Loans Commission. The government guarantee interest on the stock, but since the Public Works Loans Commission re-lend to the local authorities at a higher rate the fund is self-supporting. Should, however, a capital loss be made through a bad debt, statutory sanction has to be sought and a vote has to be taken to replace the amount, but, as a matter of fact, the government's guarantee, though frequently called, is not as a rule a burdensome liability either for interest or for principal, as the sums involved are usually not large. In recent years, however, the guarantee has become more burdensome. In the last three years sums of £70,000, £80,000 and this year £150,000 have had to be found.

In the third class comes the Guaranteed Irish Land Stock issued by various governments to buy out the Irish landlords, which might become a liability if the Irish farmers, who have bought their land on the instalment system, should fail to pay their instalments. It is remarkable, however, that in spite of the disturbed state of parts of Ireland instalments have been paid with great regularity.

Lastly, in the same class, come the two post-war expedients, Trade Facilities and Export Credits. Under the Trade Facilities Acts, 1921 to 1926, the Treasury can, on the recommendation of an advisory committee, guarantee both principal and interest on loans for capital enterprises or manufactures in the United Kingdom, if such loans are calculated to reduce unemployment. This plan is, therefore, for the encouragement of home trade: and the system of Export Credits is designed as a similar encouragement for foreign trade. The Exports Credit Guarantee Department, under the Overseas Trade Acts, 1920 to 1930, after consultation with an advisory committee, for a specified premium guarantees 75 per cent. of the face value of sterling bills drawn by exporters against goods shipped abroad which were wholly or partly produced or manufactured in the United Kingdom, within a limit of 26 million pounds.

This book is concerned only with the financial aspect of these measures. It is outside its scope to discuss whether, indeed, trade is assisted or unemployment likely to be reduced by these acts. It is sufficient to mention that their utility has been impugned. The burden that will eventually fall on the state cannot yet be accurately assessed, but it will not be very large. There has certainly been some loss, that on Export Credits so far amounting to under two millions, while on Trade Facilities up to 31st March, 1931, under a million has had to be issued from the Consolidated Fund in respect of guarantees. Whether the benefits secured will be greater than the loss incurred, time alone can show.

CHAPTER XIII

ASSETS, CONVERSION AND SINKING FUNDS

ASSETS

THE total liabilities of the state, detailed in the last chapter, were estimated on 31st March, 1931, to be approximately 7,583 millions, to which must be added some 63 millions guaranteed under the Trade Facilities Acts, and some 600 millions more of guaranteed loans of various sorts. Against such vast liabilities there are shown annually in the finance accounts the nation's estimated assets. Foremost amongst these stand 'Advances from the Exchequer un-repaid,' roughly 76 millions. The value of this asset is, however, extremely doubtful, as the chief debtor is the Unemployment Insurance Fund, and the 75 millions owed to the Treasury from that source cannot be regarded as a first-class asset. The next largest item is the estimated market value of the Suez Canal shares, 42 millions, and the shares of the Anglo-Persian Oil Company at 5 millions also appear. Various other items are specified, and, in all, the Treasury reckons the national assets to be somewhere in the neighbourhood of 168 millions, to which must be added the balance of the Exchequer Account, 6 millions. There are also some 2,300 millions owed to Great Britain by various dominions, colonies and foreign countries, but the value of many of these assets is extremely problematical. But, even including all these assets at face value, the national balance-sheet would still show: assets, 2,500 millions; liabilities (excluding contingent liabilities), 7,600 millions. This would not make a satisfactory reading for a shareholder in a joint stock company, and goes to emphasise what was said in an earlier portion of this book – that no comparison is possible between the state and an individual or a company, and that the nation's real assets lie in its taxpayers' pockets. That being so, it is clear that the greater the reserve of taxable wealth behind a nation the greater will be that nation's ability to meet all sudden stresses or strains, whereas the country that is taxed almost to the limit has little or no reserve on which to call in time of emergency. At the present, Great Britain is struggling with a colossal debt, large blocks of which are maturing each year, and some of which still bear a comparatively high rate of interest. Again and again successive Chancellors have stated that the burden of taxation cannot be satisfactorily reduced until the burden of the debt has first been lightened. Every taxpayer, therefore, has the best of reasons for seeking information as to how this can be done, and as to what steps the Treasury is taking to do it.

CONVERSION

Before starting on a consideration of how the burden of the debt can be lessened, the conditions under which the greater part of it was incurred must be restated. In Chapter XI it was made clear that the bulk of the national debt as it exists to-day was borrowed under war conditions, and it was further demonstrated that debt incurred under such conditions was likely to be of a redeemable variety, probably carrying a high rate of interest. Such is indeed the case in Great Britain to-day, and, in addition, large portions of the debt are redeemable at no very distant date. In that chapter, also, it was seen that, once peaceful and stable conditions supervened on those prevalent during the war, it was in the interests of both the Treasury and the investor that fresh bargains should be struck between them with a view to postponing the payment of the debt to as distant a time as possible. This fresh bargain was in the Treasury's interest, because it relieved it of its obligation to find large sums in cash, and it was also to the investor's interest to sacrifice his right to cash down for the right to receive a fixed interest over a long period during which interest rates seemed likely to fall. This process was known as conversion. At first sight conversion might appear to effect the very reverse of what it was intended to do, namely, to lighten the burden of the debt, since it postpones repayment and stabilises a rate of interest over a number of years. It is perfectly true that conversion does not pay off debt, but it is outside the bounds of possibility that the country could hope to pay off its debts as they matured, and by postponing repayment indefinitely the Treasury has at any rate got rid of the possible menace of the necessity of raising money for debt repayment at a time when money is very tight. Moreover, experience has shown that, once a nation's debts are converted into irredeemable loans, a scaling down of the rate of interest becomes a very much simpler task, for the government has an option but no obligation to repay. Thus in 1888 holders of Consols were asked if they would prefer to take a stock paying $2\frac{3}{4}$ per cent. for fourteen years and thereafter $2\frac{1}{2}$ per cent. in the place of their existing 3 per cent. stock, or they could be paid off at par. And such were the conditions in those happy days that the majority of holders preferred to convert.

SINKING FUNDS

Conversion of redeemable into irredeemable debt is therefore the first step in the long process of relief for the taxpayer, and the steps that have been taken in this direction since the war have already been detailed in Chapter XI. Rather special factors contributed to render the operations there discussed less favourable to the Treasury than they might have been. Amongst these handicaps was the fact that British credit did not stand very high at that moment. Before even larger conversion operations could be attempted, British credit had to be improved. Of all the methods of improving credit, a regular policy of debt redemption is the most successful. Not only does it indicate that a nation is living within its means, for the only true form of debt redemption is from surplus revenue, but capital values are steadied and investors thereby attracted. Since 1921 the British government has tried, in good years and in bad, to provide something out of revenue to go towards the reduction of debt. The money thus put aside is called a sinking fund, and it is necessary to examine this mechanism, though unfortunately, and partly from no fault of their own, the government's attempts to improve British credit, after ten years of effort, have not met with all the success that might have been expected, or, indeed, even as much as they deserved.

A sinking fund, a favourite policy of the younger Pitt, is an old and tried friend. It consists in putting aside some revenue every year in order to pay off debt.

The history of sinking funds consists chiefly in the trial of various expedients to ensure that the same amount of debt should be paid off regularly each year, but none have been found infallible. Repayment of debt is never an exciting or popular policy, and raiding the sinking fund is a favourite resource of Chancellors when they are pinched for money. But, even if sinking funds are tied up or hidden away, there is still the danger that the Treasury may be compelled to pay off debt with one hand and borrow with the other. That may or may not be an advantageous process, but it certainly does not improve the nation's credit, nor does it reduce debt. The only real sinking fund, then, is a surplus of revenue over expenditure, and, when realised, this surplus, known as the Old Sinking Fund, is, in fact, applied to the service of the debt. It is automatic. If there is a credit balance on the revenue side of the Exchequer Account at the end of the year, it goes in reduction of debt. The Exchequer Account is the Consolidated Fund. Into this all receipts should go and out of it all payments be made. But many of these entries will not be revenue of the year, for all repayments of loans, Treasury Bills, and other capital outgoings, are passed through it, and so are all capital receipts. The balance which goes in reduction of debt is the excess of revenue for the year over expenditure for the year. Revenue is taxes, customs duties and so on. Expenditure is Supply and Consolidated Fund Services. The balance only of revenue and expenditure is taken for the Old Sinking Fund, which balance may be a very different thing from that of the whole Exchequer Account.[1] This balance is struck at 4 p.m. on 31st March, on which day, it will be remembered, the country closes its accounts.

Under the Sinking Funds Act, 1875, the amount comprising the Old Sinking Fund (if any) must be issued by the Treasury to the National Debt Commissioners some time before the close of the financial year immediately following that in which it accrued. The National Debt Commissioners must have spent the money by a date not later than six months after the day on which the Treasury made the issue. Only such government stock, the interest of which is a direct and primary charge upon the Consolidated Fund, may be redeemed, save that under the Treasury Bills Act, 1877, Treasury Bills other than bills issued under Consolidated Fund or Appropriation Acts may be purchased. During the years immediately following the war the large size of the national accounts led to a change in the method of debt redemption, though it did not affect the total amount of debt redeemed. As the accumulation of large sums locked up in the Exchequer Account might have seriously disorganised the money market, the Treasury were given power to issue forthwith any surplus balance which from time to time might be available for the reduction of debt. Thus in the

[1] For the year ended 31st March, 1931, revenue amounted roughly to 857 millions, expenditure to roughly 881 millions. There was therefore no surplus for the Old Sinking Fund.

year ended 31st March, 1922, the realised surplus was over 100 millions, all of which had already, by 31st March, gone to the reduction of the debt, so that nothing accrued to the Old Sinking Fund. This fund therefore does not prove a regular and reliable debt redeemer and no very great reliance was put upon it even before the war. As might have been expected, Mr. Gladstone invented a method of debt redemption which still survives in rather a ghostly form to-day. Annuities for the reduction of the national debt were a kind of special sinking fund, since the government cancelled a certain amount of government stock and instead gave the holder, usually a government department, a terminable annuity, whereby, for a given number of years, interest plus a portion of the capital was paid each year. With the establishment of the New Sinking Fund, annuities for reduction of debt went out of fashion, and the only payments made under this head in the year ended 31st March, 1931, were £923,259 on account of principal for life annuities and annuities for terms of years, and, what is more akin to Mr. Gladstone's kind of annuity, £15,547 5*s*. on behalf of a sinking fund annuity created in 1884 to extinguish the nominal increase of capital of debt caused by the conversion of that year, and which will expire in 1934. In 1875, Sir Stafford Northcote invented a system which lasted right down to the war and has been revived since. Sir Stafford decided to devote a certain sum each year which, after defraying the cost of interest and management, was to provide a margin for the redemption of debt. This margin came to be known as the New Sinking Fund. The total cost of the service of the debt at the beginning of the war was 24 millions, which left a margin of 5¼ millions for the New Sinking Fund. During the war a general sinking fund was in abeyance, but special sinking funds were attached to various loans, of which that attached to the 5 per cent. War Loan (called the Depreciation Account), the Funding Loan and Victory Bonds Sinking Fund, the 3½ per cent. Conversion Loan Sinking Fund and the 4 per cent. Consolidated Loan Sinking Fund still survive, though now merged into the New Sinking Fund (1928).

But, though all the special sinking funds are thus merged in the New Sinking Fund, one of them has a potential importance over and above it. That is the Depreciation Account, attached to the second war loan, of which the 5 per cent. Loan is still outstanding, issued in 1917. This

one-eighth per cent. per month, or say 1½% a year, on the amount of the loan outstanding. It must be used for buying and cancelling stock whenever the market price falls below the issue price, which is 95 per cent. Sinking fund is suspended when the unexpended balance reaches 10 million pounds. Now the amount of stock on 31st March, 1931, was £2,095,952,275, and though the stock stands now over issue price, and the sinking fund is suspended, still there is a potential sinking fund at the rate of over 25 million pounds a year, if the price of the stock falls below 95. So large a discount on such a high interest-bearing security would mean dear money, the rate for Treasury Bills would be high, and under the 1928 arrangement, to be described shortly, the interest expenses of the debt would be eating into the amount available for the sinking fund. Under these circumstances the amount of the New Sinking Fund would have to be increased, for it would not then be enough to pay this new charge, and the other special sinking funds as well.

The New Sinking Fund was re-established by Mr. Baldwin in 1923, but on a completely different system. Under the Finance Act, 1923, a fixed sum was set aside every year for debt repayment, 40 million pounds for the first year, 45 million pounds for the second, and 50 million pounds for the third and every subsequent year, until the House of Commons should otherwise determine. The money had to be issued within the financial year to the National Debt Commissioners and applied by them within nine months 'in the purchasing, redeeming or paying off of debt charged on the Consolidated Fund,' excluding Ways and Means Advances, which have been described under Floating Debt.

In 1928 the New Sinking Fund underwent a further change, or, rather, a reversion to type. In that year, Mr. Churchill determined to fix an annual charge from which was to be defrayed the cost of interest, and the management and expenses of the debt, and an annual sinking fund. That charge was fixed at 355 millions a year, and it was calculated that, after provision had been made for interest, management and expenses of the debt a sufficiently large sum would be left to provide for all the statutory sinking funds, the capital payments on the American debt, together with a margin for extra debt redemption. Indeed, Mr. Churchill reckoned that even if interest rates remained as high as 4½ per cent. the whole debt, under this system, would be wiped off in exactly fifty years! Two years later, Mr. Snowden, in view of a deficit of 14½ millions on the previous year's budget, decided to add 5 millions a year to the New Sinking Fund for each of the next three years, and such a sum was indeed added in the year ended 31st March, 1931. In addition, the Finance Act of 1930 also provided that, in future, when a deficit was realised for any year, an amount equal to that of the deficit should be added to the New Sinking Fund in the following year. In 1931, however, both these provisions were abandoned, and, moreover, by the Finance No. 2 Act of that year, the permanent annual charge was reduced to 322 millions for the current and the following year. For the year ended 31st March, 1931, the total sum expended in debt reduction was nearly 67 millions, but, as there was no real surplus of revenue over expenditure, but rather the reverse, that sum does not represent the true result of the year's debt redemption operations, which, in fact, resulted in a very much smaller real reduction of debt.

Finally, the process whereby debt is redeemed may be described. First, that part of the sinking fund which is to go towards the redemption of the capital of the American debt, at present about 5 millions a year, is paid, not to the National Debt Commissioners, but to the Treasury, which by means of the Exchange Account purchases dollars throughout the year and so is enabled to pay its debt to the American Treasury at Washington without unduly disturbing the exchange markets. The remainder of the fund is issued from time to time to the National Debt Commissioners.

The National Debt Commissioners buy stock and cancel it. They employ a well-known firm of stockbrokers known as the Government Brokers, who of course buy prudently, so as to avoid raising the price against themselves, and they take advantage of every fall in value. The actual amount of day-to-day purchases is settled in consultation between them and the National Debt Commissioners. Only stocks directly charged upon the Consolidated Fund can be bought, not stocks for which we are merely guarantors, such as Local Loans or Guaranteed Irish Land Stock. When stock is bought, the entry in the books at the Bank of England is cancelled and the operation is complete. The country is free from so much more debt.

APPENDIX I

FINANCE BILLS

CERTIFIED UNDER PARLIAMENT ACT

1913. 1914. 1914–15 (No. 1). 1916 (New Duties).
1919. 1920. 1922. 1925. 1926. 1928–9. 1930–1.

NOT CERTIFIED UNDER PARLIAMENT ACT

1914–15 (No. 2). 1914–15 (No. 3). 1916. 1917–18.
1918. 1921. 1923. 1924. 1927. 1928. 1929–30.

TITLES OF BILLS, OTHER THAN FINANCE BILLS, CERTIFIED AS MONEY BILLS UNDER PARLIAMENT ACT

Provisional Collection of Taxes.
Government of Soudan Loan.
Public Buildings Expenses.
Isle of Man (Customs).
Telegraph (Money).
Anglo-Persian Oil Company (Acquisition of Capital).
East African Protectorates (Loan).
War Loan.
Death Duties (Killed in War).
Superannuation.
War Loan Extension.
Police Magistrates (Superannuation).
American Loan.
Army Annual Act, 1916, Amendment.
Government War Obligations.
Representation of the People (Returning Officers' Expenses).
Civil Contingencies Fund.
Disabled Men (Facilities for Employment).
Retired Officers (Civil Employment).
Superannuation (Prison Officers).

Resident Magistrates (Ireland).
British Empire Exhibition (Guarantee).
Mr. Speaker's Retirement.
Housing (Scotland) (No. 2).
Land Settlement Amendment.
Safeguarding of Industries.
Irish Railways (Settlement of Claims).
Diseases of Animals.
Anglo-Persian Oil Company (Payment of Calls).
West Indian Islands (Telegraph).
Old Age Pensions.
Irish Free State Land Purchase (Loan Guarantee).
War Charges (Validity).
China Indemnity (Application).
Palestine and East Africa Loans (Guarantee).
Overseas Trade.
Pensions (Governors of Dominions).
Unemployment Insurance.
Air Transport (Subsidy Agreements).
Highlands and Islands (Medical Service) Additional Grant.

APPENDIX II

Example of an Appropriation Account

CIVIL APPROPRIATION ACCOUNTS, 1929

BRITISH MUSEUM

ACCOUNT of the Sum Expended, in the Year ended 31st March, 1930, compared with the Sum Granted, for the Salaries and other Expenses of the BRITISH MUSEUM, including certain Grant in Aid.

Service	Grant	Expenditure			Expenditure compared with Grant					
					Less than Granted.			More than Granted.		
BRITISH MUSEUM.	£	£	s.	d.	£	s.	d.	£	s.	d.
A.—Salaries, Wages, and Allowances	137,087	137,277	18	11	—			190	18	11
B.—Police Pensioners and Police	6,612	6,712	7	11	—			100	7	11
C.—Purchases and Acquisitions (Grant in Aid)	25,000	25,000	0	0	—			—		
D.—Mounting, Preparing, etc.	1,600	1,351	10	7	248	9	5	—		
E.—Printing, Photography, etc.	13,175	13,210	7	0	—			35	7	0
F.—Fire-Extinguishing Apparatus	250	230	1	6	19	18	6	—		
G.—Furniture and Fittings ..	6,000	6,013	4	9	—			13	4	9
H.—Incidental Expenses ..	6,198	6,073	5	3	124	14	9	—		
I.—Telephones	550	568	4	11	—			18	4	11
J.—Annuity in respect of Loan for Purchase of Land (57 & 58 Vict. c. 34)	7,733	7,732	10	0		10	0	—		
TOTAL, BRITISH MUSEUM £	204,205	204,169	10	10	393	12	8	358	3	6

EXPLANATION of the Causes of Variation between Expenditure and Grant.

B.—Excess due to an increase in the rate of pay of Police Pensioners for Sunday duty.

D.—The expenditure on materials was below the average.

INDEX

Bei Fragen zur Produktsicherheit wenden Sie sich bitte an:
If you have any questions regarding product safety,
please contact:

Walter de Gruyter GmbH
Genthiner Straße 13
10785 Berlin
productsafety@degruyterbrill.com